Tastes & Tales of Norway

Hippocrene is NUMBER ONE in International Cookbooks

Africa and Oceania
Best of Regional African Cooking
Egyptian Cooking
Good Food from Australia
Traditional South African Cookery
Taste of Eritrea

Asia and Near East
The Best of Taiwanese Cuisine
Imperial Mongolian Cooking
The Joy of Chinese Cooking
The Best of Regional Thai Cuisine
Japanese Home Cooking
Healthy South Indian Cooking
The Indian Spice Kitchen
Best of Goan Cooking
Best of Kashmiri Cooking
Afghan Food and Cookery
The Art of Persian Cooking
The Art of Turkish Cooking
The Art of Uzbek Cooking

Mediterranean
Best of Greek Cuisine
Taste of Malta
A Spanish Family Cookbook
Tastes of North Africa

Western Europe
Art of Dutch Cooking
Best of Austrian Cuisine
A Belgian Cookbook
Cooking in the French Fashion (bilingual)
Celtic Cookbook
Cuisines of Portuguese Encounters
English Royal Cookbook
The Swiss Cookbook
Traditional Recipes from Old England
The Art of Irish Cooking
Feasting Galore Irish-Style
Traditional Food from Scotland
Traditional Food from Wales
The Scottish-Irish Pub and Hearth Cookbook
A Treasury of Italian Cuisine (bilingual)

Scandinavia
Best of Scandinavian Cooking
The Best of Finnish Cooking
The Best of Smorgasbord Cooking
Good Food from Sweden
Tastes & Tales of Norway
Icelandic Food & Cookery

Central Europe
All Along the Rhine
All Along the Danube
Best of Albanian Cooking
Best of Croatian Cooking
Bavarian Cooking
Traditional Bulgarian Cooking
The Best of Czech Cooking
The Best of Slovak Cooking
The Art of Hungarian Cooking
Hungarian Cookbook
Art of Lithuanian Cooking
Polish Heritage Cookery
The Best of Polish Cooking
Old Warsaw Cookbook
Old Polish Traditions
Treasury of Polish Cuisine (bilingual)
Poland's Gourmet Cuisine
The Polish Country Kitchen Cookbook
Taste of Romania
Taste of Latvia

Eastern Europe
The Best of Russian Cooking
Traditional Russian Cuisine (bilingual)
The Best of Ukrainian Cuisine

Americas
A Taste of Quebec
Argentina Cooks
Cooking the Caribbean Way
Mayan Cooking
The Honey Cookbook
The Art of Brazilian Cookery
The Art of South American Cookery
Old Havana Cookbook (bilingual)

Tastes & Tales of Norway

SIRI LISE DOUB

photographs by
INGER-LISE SKAAR AND GILL HOLLAND

HIPPOCRENE BOOKS, INC.
New York

Also by Siri Lise Doub:
Taste of Latvia

For information, address:
HIPPOCRENE BOOKS, INC.
171 Madison Avenue
New York, NY 10016

Cataloging-in-Publication Data available from the Library of Congress.

ISBN 0-7818-0877-4

Printed in the United States of America.

Where do you find more blue the sky?
Where do more merrily
The brooks run through the meadow
To bathe the many flowers?
Even winter gives me joy,
As bright and clear as were it strewn
With lily petals all in white
And with the splendour of the starry vault.

—Henrik Wergeland from
Milestones of Norwegian Literature

꩜

Acknowledgements

*T*his book would not have been possible without the advice, assistance, encouragement, and expertise of my aunt Inger-Lise, who charmed Norwegians across Norway into contributing recipes, stories, tours, hotel rooms, and meals for this book. She shows us the nooks and crannies of Norway as only she can.

In addition, much admiration and thanks go to my parents. My father contributed photographs and translations as well as much-needed advice and delight. Not only did my mother contribute her expertise and invaluable advice and assistance in the kitchen, but she gently teaches all of us the hospitality, warmth, and generosity at the root of Norwegian culture. Special thanks to Hans Jacob and Johnny. My Norwegian family, my mormor, Tante Kjærsti, Onkel Bjørn, Vibeke, Monica, Bjørn, Wenche, Kåre, Tante Bjørg, and Onkel Per have all also been instrumental in the writing of this book.

Much love and thanks to my extraordinary husband Robb, who has already shown me adventures enough for several lifetimes. I look forward to many more. Also to my brother Gill, who not only keeps the warm tradition of Norwegian hospitality alive and well in the city but bravely coerced many of his Norwegian friends to contribute to these pages. And finally much thanks and admiration for my sweet sister Astri, who provides constant love and support to our family. All give me strength and encouragement.

Grateful acknowledgement is also made to the Doub family, the Kollme family, Carol Chitnis-Gress, Anne Greta Forde, Stian at Bryggehotel, Joan Werness Martin, D.L. Ashliman, Lisa Anne Yayla, Lisbeth at Lofoton Destination, Anne Senstad, Nina Koren, Lars Alldén of Aschehoug Publishing, Per at Ullerns Hotel, Ola, Gerd Hatlem, Bjornar Larsen, Trude Solheim, Jan Horn, Roger Tømmerås, Terry Forshaw, Elisabeth Seljevold, Grand Hotel Terminus, Geir Midtun, Bent Larsen, Edmund Harris Utne, Hanne Svärd of the Norwegian Meat Marketing Board, Arne Gjermundsen of Ministry of Foreign Affairs; Kjeld Karlsen and Steinar Anderson of NOR-MEDIA AS, and Joanna Yas of Open City.

*For Mormor
and my Norwegian family*

Table of Contents

Introduction

$\mathcal{A}$rne Brimi, master chef at the Fossheim Turisthotell in the tiny mountain community of Lom, captured the spirit of Norwegian culture and cuisine in *The Norseman*: "Flavors should be pure and not overpower each other. Food should satisfy all of our senses." Such natural purity exemplifies Norway. A foreign officer was once posted in the hills of Norway. Surprised to find the dining hall empty when he went in to socialize before dinner, he was told that the Norwegian officers had gone for a hike. A local explained: "The mountains are there. It would be a waste not to walk up them at least once a day."

Norwegians take great pride in their country. Its pure, raw beauty is captivating indeed, but Norway's real charm lies in its people. Farmers and fishermen have toiled against a barren landscape and freezing winters for thousands of years. Yes, it is cold. But the Norwegians embrace the cold with as much vigor as they do their short, bright summers. It is the climate and terrain of Norway that have shaped the national character of the hardy Northmen. What was once a daily struggle against the elements to secure food and lodging has evolved into an appreciation of life, nature, and land found in few countries. *Norge er et deilig land* (Norway is a wonderful country) was practically the first phrase my husband ever learned from my Norwegian family.

"We Norwegians are still hunters, while the rest of the world is in the throes of forgetting where food comes from," continues Arne. Food remains simple in Norway. The coast continues to provide a comfortable diet, including seal, whale, seabirds, and eggs, as it did the country's first inhabitants. The countryside reaps delicate plant and animal life, a resource discovered as people traveled farther and farther inland and learned to cultivate the soil. In the countryside Norwegians still slaughter animals in the autumn. Meat and fish are still preserved using the salt, sugar, drying and smoking methods used for centuries.

While writing this book I have loved studying the culture and customs of my mother's land. Not only have I finally learned to create the delicious dishes that I've enjoyed for years, but I now realize that many of my favorite family customs are uniquely Norwegian. Take note before you travel there. The Norwegians, for example, are a people serious about their *skål* (toasts). When the guests at a table raise their glasses to toast, they meet every eye before taking a sip of drink. Individual toasts between two or more guests at a table are also encouraged; again, you must meet every eye. Finally, it is poor taste to toast the hostess, for if she were to toast with everyone at the table, dinner would never be served.

Norwegians eat well and are proud of it. The country's chefs have long excelled in international competitions, and even in remote parts of Norway you'll find fabulous cooks. I highly recommend you take part in the traditional feasts offered in many parts of the country. The Borg museum in Lofoten, for example, offers a Viking feast. Geilo's thirteenth-century Hol church hosts an old-fashioned Norwegian banquet on the first weekend in August every year.

Here are a few things to keep in mind as you try the recipes listed in these pages. First, gas ovens usually cook faster than electric ones. When using a gas oven, it is sometimes better to reduce heat so that your dish doesn't brown on the outside before it has actually finished cooking. As the Norwegians say, "Rather a bit correctly than much incorrectly." Also chefs have noted a difference when you use Fleischmann packaged yeast compared to traditional caked yeast. Because caked yeast rises faster, you might find that you need more yeast if you use Fleischmann yeast. Also stores in Norway rarely sell salted butter. I recommend using unsalted butter for Norwegian recipes. Specialty ingredients like vanilla sugar and vanilla sauce called for in some recipes can be ordered from many of the companies listed at the end of the book. Haram-Christensen Corp., for example, carries both products.

Finally, some recipes call for raw eggs. Keep in mind that *salmonella enteritidis*, which can cause serious illness, is sometimes found in raw eggs. Although the risk is low, I recommend that you choose the freshest eggs possible and store them at temperatures below 40° F. Serve or chill the dishes immediately. If you prefer, you may substitute pasteurized liquid eggs or dried egg whites.

At the end of the book is a list of places in the United States that provide traditional Norwegian cooking utensils. With more Norwegians here than in Norway, opportunities for shopping for Norwegian handicrafts and equipment—and for learning more about the country, its people, and its culture—are everywhere. My sister Astri studies Norwegian every week with a Norwegian in Baltimore. My brother visits regularly with Norwegian artists and photographers in New York and Los Angeles. And of course the Midwest is home to thousands of Norwegians. A particularly good resource is the Scandinavian House, 56-58 Park Avenue, New York, which displays Scandinavian culture and even has a children's learning center. Also good is the Sons of Norway website, www.sofn.com.

I hope this book serves to introduce readers not only to Norwegian cuisine but also to the vibrant culture and history of the country.

Velkommen til bords! Welcome to the table.

The Trumpet of Nordland

Greeting

I greet you, my Nordland's inhabitants, friends,
From host of the house to the poor hired man,
Be greeted my people of Nordland!

Be greeted, my yeoman, in tunics homespun,
The men of the seashore and others beyond,
Be greeted my people of Nordland!

My greetings to you who are drying the fish
And salting the cod in the barrel to ship,
Be greeted each man and each woman!

Be greeted you priesthood, both prelate and clerk,
Who serve in God's sanctified, light-giving kirk,
Each in his position important.

And also you trustworthy officers all,
Who carry the sword for the law to uphold,
From violent deeds us protecting.

Hail even to cottar and menial churl,
To landowner and those who dwell on the shore
And others, too many to mention.

Hail to our fair women beloved indeed,
All mothers and wives and young maidenhood sweet;
Your labor and virtue I honor.

I greet you and offer my services small:
I ask you to come to our house one and all
At noon when the sun is the brightest,

To do me the favor of being my guests
And grace this my table but modestly decked
According to means and position.

Elaborate dishes from countries afar,
Or bright centerpieces with glitter and star,
My pocketbook will not allow me.

Nor will there be any immoderate drink
Beyond what you custom and courtesy think;
No toast to the honor of Bacchus.

I never was trained in the kitchen of kings,
Have never had chefs to this learning me bring;
No potage of France can I make you.

And you will forgive me if I do not strike
The perfect proportion, ingredients right;
I am not a cook for the masters.

Here is no profusion from banquets of old,
No king Ahasverus both regal and bold,
No melons need here be expected.

No pheasants or doves will be found on the trays;
My bag is too light; I such role cannot play;
No capons or turkeys I bring you.

And we cannot serve you with condiments rich,
No spices from India, relish or such,
No grapes or the like to be given.

A dish is prepared of unwatered saithe,
And if it may please you to have it this day,
Partake of it with my good wishes.

A plateful of butter before you will stand,
Of barley-made flatbread some loaves are at hand;
Each take what his heart may desire.

Of such as we have, there is plenty to share;
Our winter-made sausages will not be spared,
Nor watered-down milk for the thirsty.

A ham in the storehouse I still have retained.
Nine autumns in smoke it has even remained
And ought to be cured, I am thinking.

A barrel of herring I have in my store,
Has been well soured a season or more,
I fry you a couple with pleasure.

For olives and pickles and melons, the like,
I give you but cabbage; it has to suffice;
I have nothing further to offer.

My salad a mush, made of turnip, will be;
No candied lemon in my house you see;
Our fare is but modest and simple.

Yet lefse and sweet cheese in plenty is here.
And pancakes of eggs will be our dessert,
To speak nothing of our blood sausage.

Now once more I crave your indulgence to plead
My will must be honored in lieu of the deed
If something is not quite in order.

You notice, my dear good and honored friends.
Without further mention what here I intend
To give you in following pages.

I am to describe how our Nordland is seen,
With mountains and ocean and shoreline between,
With farms and with attributes many.

I write of the rocks and the peaks up above,
Old, troll-like and gray, with hard snow on the domes,
Of hills and of rivers and valleys;

How farmers a livelihood make here up north,
What food and what drink they set forth on the board,
And many another true feature.

Such writing, if it does not satisfy thirst
Or hunger, may give you a moment of mirth;
What more can this author you promise?

—Petter Dass, 1739 (trans. 1954)

Koldt Bord
the cold buffet

and

Smørbrød
open-faced sandwiches

O du som metter liten fugl
Vi takke deg, O Gud.

Oh you who feed the little birds
We thank you, O God.

— Old Norwegian blessing

*B*efore you can truly appreciate the *koldt bord* for which Norway is known throughout the world, you must first understand the tradition of Norwegian meals. As in the days of the Vikings, who enjoyed two main meals of *dagverd* and *nattverd*, modern Norwegians also enjoy two main meals: a large breakfast, *frokost*, and a hot *middag*. To tide them over in between are a light lunch and, in the evening, *aftens*.

Frokost is hearty, especially for special occasions. You can have as many as thirty different dishes on your breakfast table, including boiled eggs, stewed fruit, bowls of fresh berries, waffles, smoked salmon, jars of pickled herring, homemade preserves, home-baked breads and rolls, even cakes. *Spekemat*, cured meats and sausages made from salted, smoked, and matured reindeer, lamb, mutton, and other meats, figure prominently, as do the *smørbrød* fixings like cheeses, fish, and jam. Porridges like *havre-grynsgrøt* and other cereals are also popular. Wash it all down with freshly brewed coffee and jugs of fresh and specially soured milk. If there isn't enough time for quite this feast, a Norwegian will probably enjoy several thick slices of homemade bread with *geitost* (see page 29) or *syltetøy* (jam).

Although lunch for working Norwegians is usually a light sandwich of cold meats or fish and cheese, a buffet lunch table served at restaurants or for parties groans with an assortment of dishes. Added to the breakfast menu are fish and shellfish, dried meats with side dishes, and salads.

Middag, served at around 5 P.M., is generally the only hot meal of the day. Popular dishes include *kjøttkaker, får i kål, fiskeboller,* and *lapskaus.* On Saturdays before enjoying a late *aftens* you might have a light supper of the special Norwegian sour heavy cream and rice porridge or *risengrynsgrøt* (see page 260) sprinkled with raisins.

If I could, I would live only on *aftens,* by far my favorite meal of the day. Since Norwegians typically dine on *middag* early, they often enjoy a light snack before bed. This is *aftens. Aftens,* my aunt once explained to me, is whatever you have in the house. When considering Norwegian cupboards, you can be certain it'll be tasty, filling, and something to do with fish. It can include everything from scrambled eggs or a fried egg, shrimp salad, sliced cucumbers, and tomatoes to caviar and sliced smoked salmon with lemon and dill. If you've got *spekemat* in the house, you'll add an assortment of it to the table as well. Although the meal sounds very much like breakfast, it is decidedly not the same. For example, I'm told that breakfast includes boiled eggs. *Aftens* never would.

The *koldt bord* (cold table), which is held deep in Norwegian tradition, combines all these meals. Known also by its Swedish name *smørgåsbord*, the *koldt bord* is laden with meats, cheeses, and breads and is prepared for whoever might stop by. *Spekemat*, sliced paper thin, is served with cold scrambled eggs with chives, sour cream, and flatbread. Stewed potatoes with dill (see page 146) or baked potatoes with butter or sour cream sauce (see page 23) are good. Omelets are favorites. And don't forget flatbread, lingonberries, Jarlsberg cheese, and mushrooms fried in butter. Other simple dishes include vegetable trays, melons, *lefse* (see page 174), and bread.

The word *pålegg* means generally "something to put on bread": cheese, sardines, cucumbers, jam, or *spekemat*. Many of these sandwich spreads are also part of the *koldt bord;* various *smørbrød*, the famous open-faced sandwiches, are made from the table.

Above all, remember the art to dining by buffet. It is considered poor taste to load up your plate with an assortment of foods. Take your time. Begin with the cured herring. Take a new plate and try the salads and the meat. Finally, enjoy the cheese.

The next few pages offer a sampling of the dishes that make the *koldt bord* such a favorite around the world.

Breakfast at Henningsvær Bryggehotel.

🦢

> *One's own house is best, though small it may be;*
> *each man is master at home;*
> *though he have but two goats and a bark-thatched hut*
> *'tis better than craving a boon.*
>
> —Håvamål, *The Poetic Edda,*
> translated by Olive Bray,
> edited by D.L. Ashliman

*F*ish dishes figure prominently on the *koldt bord,* and herring tops the list. The following *spekesild,* or salted herring, was for many years the standby of less affluent Norwegians. For centuries it was the mainstay for many Norwegian towns, including Stavanger (see page 61) and Bodø, the largest town inside the Arctic Circle.

During the war, my mormor tells me, they ate herring and boiled potatoes daily. Today herring is no cheaper than other fish, and you'll find it at every table in Norway. Still a Saturday favorite on the west coast, it is served with onion slices, pickled beets, and boiled potatoes.

❧

Crisp Fried Herring

*F*resh herring is also good when rolled in beaten egg and bread crumbs and fried in oil.

3 herring
½ cup flour
1 tablespoon salt
1 tablespoon pepper
butter

1. Cut the head off the herring. Clean the fish.
2. Mix the flour, salt, and pepper together. Coat the fish with the flour mixture.
3. Fry in butter over medium heat.

Serve with potatoes and sour cream. Also good with beets.

MAKES 3 SERVINGS.

*S*maller than its North Sea relative, Baltic herring is known as *strømning* north of Sweden's Kalmarsund waterway. In southern Norway it is called *sild*. Both Baltic and North Sea herrings are popular fried, salted, marinated, and smoked. You'll find small buckets of salted herring or herring in brine in every supermarket in Norway. If you buy your herring this way, be sure to soak the herring in fresh water to remove the salt.

You can pickle and marinate both salted and the unsalted herring. The *matjes* herring, sold around the globe, can also be substituted for salted herring. You do not need to presoak *matjes*.

❧

Marinated Herring

sursild

4 salted herring
1 tablespoon peppercorns
1 tablespoon mustard seeds
8 to 10 cloves
5 or 6 allspice berries
1 bay leaf
2 or 3 large onions, sliced into very thin rings
1 cup vinegar (7% strength)
1½ cups sugar

1. Soak the herring in water to cover for 1 to 2 hours. Rinse well. Fillet and cut into ½-inch strips.
2. Mix the peppercorns, mustard seeds, cloves, allspice berries, and bay leaf together. Add the onion and herring.
3. Mix the vinegar, 2 cups cold water, and sugar together. Stir until sugar has dissolved.
4. Pour the vinegar marinade over the herring. Refrigerate overnight.

MAKES 4 SERVINGS.

❧
Herring in Tomato Sauce

3 or 4 salted herring (6 to 8 fillets)
½ cup tomato ketchup
½ cup soybean oil
2 tablespoons vinegar (5% strength)
2 tablespoons sugar
1 onion, chopped fine
2 pickling cucumbers, chopped fine
1 bay leaf
a few cloves

1. Soak the herring for 1 or 2 hours in water to cover. Clean and fillet.
2. Dry the herring well and cut into small pieces.
3. Mix the ketchup, oil, and vinegar until you have a smooth sauce.
4. Season to taste with sugar.
5. Mix the herring and tomato sauce. Add the onion and cucumber.
6. Mix well. Add the bay leaf and the cloves.
7. Refrigerate for about a week.

MAKES ABOUT 3 SERVINGS.

Janson's Temptation

1 onion, chopped
butter for sautéing
4 raw potatoes, sliced thinly
8 fillets of anchovy
1 cup heavy cream
2 tablespoons butter

Preheat oven to 400° F.

1. Sauté onion in butter.
2. Layer potatoes, anchovy, and sautéed onions in a greased baking dish.
3. Pour cream over entire dish. Dot with butter.
4. Bake about 45 minutes. Serve very hot.

MAKES 4 SERVINGS.

⚬

Herring in Mustard Sauce

sild i sennep

1½ cups diluted vinegar (2 parts water, 3 parts 5% vinegar)
5 or 6 tablespoons sugar
1 tablespoon mustard
4 fillets of herring
1 small onion, chopped
1 carrot, chopped
2 bay leaves
allspice

1. Mix vinegar, sugar, and mustard. Bring to a boil over medium heat.
2. Layer herring, onion, carrot, bay leaves, and allspice until all ingredients have been used.
3. Pour vinegar mixture over the herring. Refrigerate until served.

MAKES 4 SERVINGS.

❧
Herring and Egg Salad

5 fillets of herring
3 eggs, hard-boiled
1 cup *rømme* (see page 23)
about 1 teaspoon sugar
lemon juice
dill and parsley

1. Cut herring in small pieces. Cut eggs into small pieces.
2. Whisk *rømme* with sugar.
3. Add lemon juice to taste.
4. Mix herring and egg. Blend with *rømme* mix.
5. Garnish with plenty of dill and parsley.

MAKES 4 SERVINGS.

❧

Herring, Beet, and Apple Salad

1 salted herring
1½ cups cooked and diced beets
½ cup cooked and diced potatoes
½ cup cooked and diced carrots
1 cup cooked and diced meat (beef, pork, or veal)
2 apples, diced
1 dill pickle, diced
3 eggs, hard-boiled

MARINADE

pepper
1 cup heavy cream
3 tablespoons vinegar
1 teaspoon prepared mustard
½ teaspoon salt
2 tablespoons sugar

1. Wash herring and soak overnight in cold water.
2. Drain. Cut off head and tail and remove the bones.
3. Cut the fillets into small pieces. Mix lightly with diced beets, potatoes, and carrots. Add meat, apples, and pickle. Chop 2 of the hard-boiled eggs and add in, mixing well.
4. Mix the ingredients for the marinade together. Pour over the herring mixture.
5. Season to taste.
6. Garnish with parsley and slices of the remaining hard-boiled egg.

MAKES 4 SERVINGS.

❧
Smoked Salmon with Scrambled Eggs

*I*n Norway smoked salmon, or *røkelaks*, often accompanies scrambled eggs. The salmon is usually smoked for 8 hours in cold smoke. Most fishermen send their catch away to smoking houses to be smoked.

Plan for about ⅓ pound of salmon per person. Cut the smoked salmon in very thin slices. Arrange in overlapping slices on a dish with the scrambled eggs. Garnish with fresh dill or parsley. Serve at room temperature.

Røkelaks is also delicious with scrambled eggs on an open-faced sandwich.

❧
Eggerøre

scrambled eggs

4 eggs
3 tablespoons heavy cream or whole milk
salt
1 or 2 tablespoons chives
1½ tablespoons butter
tomato wedges
parsley

1. Beat eggs. Mix well with cream, salt, and chives.
2. Melt the butter in a medium-hot frying pan. Add the egg mixture.
3. Gently heat the mixture. Stir occasionally until scrambled.
4. Remove to platter and decorate with tomato wedges and parsley.

MAKES 4 SERVINGS.

❧
Caviar and Egg Plate

Serve each ingredient separately in small dishes. Your guests can serve themselves a tablespoon or two of each ingredient on a plate.

1 tablespoon red trout or salmon caviar
1 tablespoon yellow capelin caviar
1 tablespoon black caviar
1 egg, hard-boiled, segmented
a dollop of *rømme* (see page 23)
1 tablespoon chopped red onion

Serve with flatbread, butter, and a glass of beer.

MAKES 1 SERVING.

❧
Capelin Roe

1 tablespoon capelin roe
1 tablespoon chopped white onion
1 tablespoon chopped red onion
1 teaspoon chopped chives
a dollop sour cream

Serve as you would the caviar plate (above).

MAKES 1 SERVING.

*T*he sour cream used so often as a side dish in Norway has a unique taste that comes from soured milk. My morfar adored the thick cream. He set aside whole milk and left it for several days to sour. When the surface of the milk thickened, he sprinkled bread crumbs and sugar on it and ate the cream with a spoon. Sour cream usually accompanies fish.

❧

Sour Heavy Cream Sauce

rømme

1½ cups heavy cream
5 tablespoons chopped dill
juice of ½ lemon
1 teaspoon sugar
pinch of white pepper

1. Whip the cream, dill, lemon juice, sugar, and pepper together.
2. Refrigerate until serving.

MAKES 5 SERVINGS.

⚘
Whole Glazed Trout

1 whole trout, about 3 pounds
2 tablespoons salt
1 bay leaf
8 peppercorns
1 slice lemon
2½ cups fish stock
1 packet powdered aspic
lemon slices, parsley, and fresh dill

1. Place the fish in a pan that will hold it in a semicircle. Place the fish, backbone up, in the pan. Cover with water. Add salt, bay leaf, peppercorns, lemon, and fish stock. Bring to a boil. Skim off any fat the rises to the top.
2. Reduce heat and let simmer for about 8 minutes. Remove from heat. Set aside to cool.
3. When you are ready to serve the fish, dissolve the aspic in a few tablespoons of water. Remove the fish from the stock and cut along the back fins, around the tail, and around the head.
4. Pull the skin carefully off the body. Do not remove from tail and head. Remove the strip of fat along the back fins. Let the fish drain before placing it on a serving dish. When the aspic begins to thicken, brush the entire fish with aspic.
5. Garnish with lemon slices, parsley, and fresh dill.

MAKES 4 SERVINGS.

People can never know enough about others to judge rightly.

—Sigrid Undset, Norwegian historical novelist
and author of *Kristin Lavransdatter,* winner of
the Nobel Prize for Literature in 1928

❧

Crab Salad with Coriander

1 head lettuce, shredded
1½ cups whipping cream
¾ cup crème fraîche
1 onion, finely chopped
1 cup finely chopped peeled, deseeded tomatoes
3 shallots, chopped
fresh coriander (optional)
meat from 2 crabs
parsley (optional)

1. Place the lettuce in a bowl.
2. Whip the cream. Mix it with crème fraîche.
3. Add the onion, tomatoes, and shallots to cream mixture. Mix lightly. Add a little coriander if desired. Add crabmeat.
4. Pour the mixture over the lettuce.
5. Garnish with fresh coriander or parsley.

MAKES 3 OR 4 SERVINGS.

*H*eavier than smoked salmon, *gravlaks,* which is salmon lightly salted and allowed to ferment, is often served as a meal rather than a snack. Another form of fermented fish is *rakefisk,* which is partially fermented fish like trout, salmon, herring, and even shark. In the old days the fish was salted and then buried underground to ferment. It is served with boiled potatoes, *lefse,* and butter. *Rakefisk* has become increasingly popular in recent years, with groups like *Rakefiskens Venneklubb* (Friends of Rakefisk) to promote it.

For a less complicated mustard sauce, mix 1 cup mayonnaise with 2 tablespoons mustard.

❦

Marinated Salmon

gravlaks

2 pounds frozen salmon
1 tablespoon salt
1 tablespoon sugar
1 teaspoon white pepper
dill

MUSTARD SAUCE

2 tablespoons any mild mustard
1 egg yolk
1 tablespoon sugar
1½ tablespoons vinegar
1 cup soybean oil
fresh dill, finely chopped

1. Fillet the fish when it is almost fully thawed, but not quite. (It is easier to slice if you don't remove the skin.) If you buy fresh fillets, freeze for a day before preparing.

2. Mix the salt, sugar, and pepper together. Rub the mixture into the salmon. Rub as much dill as desired into the fish.

3. Place the fillets in pairs, skin sides facing each other, in a large dish on a bed of dill mixed with any remaining salt, sugar, and pepper. Cover with a cheesecloth and place a light weight on them. Refrigerate for 2 or 3 days, turning twice a day.

4. To make the mustard sauce, beat the mustard, egg yolk, and sugar together. Mix the vinegar and oil. Add slowly to the egg and mustard mixture until sauce is thick and smooth. Add dill to taste.

Serve the salmon in thin slices. Garnish with fresh dill. Serve with mustard sauce and stewed potatoes (see page 146) for dinner. Serve as canapés or with brown bread for lunch.

MAKES 4 SERVINGS.

NORWEGIAN DAIRY PRODUCTS

$\mathcal{A}$ popular legend from Seljord, home of elves and serpents, tells the tale of Strong Nils, whose strength was credited to the fact that he was suckled on mare's milk. A large boulder bears the plaque, "This stone, weighing 570 kilos, was lifted by Strong Nils, 1722–1800." His house stands by the path nearby.

Whether the tale of Nils is true or not, the attributes of milk were widely known in Norway. Moreover, milk was used to make butter, one of the most coveted Norwegian units of currency in the days of a barter economy. Butter once had such high status that at weddings it was molded into large pyramidal sculptures and placed on the table as a decoration. The original hand-carved wooden molds are on display in ethnological museums across the country. Butter was also much appreciated during World War II. My great grandparents traded eggs from the chickens they kept for just a morsel of the precious stuff.

In addition to butter, milk became cheese, buttermilk, and quite an extraordinary variety of other dairy products. *Syra*, for example, is an ancient dairy drink still popular today. This soured whey is the thin, watery part of the milk that separates from the curds when milk curdles. *Rørost* was also made from soured milk. Milk is stirred until thin and then placed over low heat and warmed. When the milk curdles, the curds are removed and the whey extracted from them. Soured milk is also used in a barley or oat porridge.

Norwegians also enjoy sour milk cheese (*gammelost*), which is made by boiling milk without adding rennet. *Gammelost* (literally "old cheese") was only truly *gammel* after it had matured for ten years. It was believed to prevent sickness and infection. The young girls on the *seter* made the *gammelost* every June. It is made from skim milk, which is left to sour in large wooden buckets and then heated in a large cast-iron pot. The separated curds are placed in a mold, and the whey drained through a cheesecloth and fed to the animals or cooked down to *prim ost*. (*Prim* itself was a soft, sweet, whey cheese. Maren Elisabet Bang gives a recipe for it in her famous nineteenth-century cookbook *Everyman's Book of Housekeeping*.) The drained cheese was placed on a warm shelf in the cabin and taken to the farm when the girls returned in the fall. By Christmas the cheese had fermented and was ready to eat. Today *gammelost* is produced in modern factories.

Geitost, brown goat's cheese, has a unique taste. Although many say it is an acquired taste, I find it to be rich and absolutely delicious. I have noticed it popping up in such specialty stores like Dean & Deluca in America. *Geitost* is especially good on *knekkebrød* or thickly buttered dark bread. The cheese is still made on farms in Norway. Storhaugen, for example, is one farm that specializes in producing goat milk. Situated on Norway's highest mountain, Galdhøpiggen (2469 meters, 8100 feet), Storhaugen is worth a visit. It allows a spectacular view of the Jotunheim mountains in the Jotunheimen National Park ("Home of the Giants") and is a good base for summer skiing on the Juv glacier.

In the old days some housewives also added milk to beef and pork stews. *Kalvedans* ("calf dance"), for example, was a kind of milk pudding or veal brawn. A Vesteraalen recipe calls for boiling the head and hooves of the calf and chopping the meat fine. Boil in milk and barley and when it has cooled, carve and serve.

The Synnøve Finden cheese was first produced on this farm.

✶
Jarlsberg Cheese and Smoked Salmon Appetizer

4 slices smoked salmon
4 large, thin slices of Jarlsberg cheese
chopped celery
chopped dill

1. Place a slice of salmon on a slice of cheese. Sprinkle with celery and dill. Fold it nicely together.
2. Continue with other slices of cheese and salmon.

Serve with crisp lettuce, bread, and butter.

MAKES 4 SERVINGS.

✶
Cheese and Ham Omelet

4 eggs
½ teaspoon salt
butter for frying
1 cup grated Swiss or Jarlsberg cheese
4 ounces ham or smoked sausage, chopped
1 leek, diced

1. Beat the eggs, 4 tablespoons water, and salt together. Melt butter in a frying pan over low to medium heat. Pour in egg mixture.
2. Scatter the cheese, ham or sausage, and leek over the eggs.
3. Cover and leave for 6 to 8 minutes.

MAKES ABOUT 4 SERVINGS.

❧❧
Summer Salad

DRESSING

1½ cups heavy whipping cream
¾ cup mayonnaise
1 bunch chives
½ bulb fennel, chopped, or 1 bunch fresh watercress, chopped
½ cup chopped almonds
coarsely ground pepper

SALAD

4 eggs
1 red lettuce
6 tomatoes, sliced
½ cucumber, sliced
1 bunch radishes, sliced
5 ounces Jarlsberg cheese, diced
5 ounces boiled ham, cut in strips

1. First, make the dressing. Whip the cream. Mix cream and mayonnaise. Add chives, fennel or watercress, almonds, and pepper. Mix well. Set aside.
2. Boil the eggs for 8 to 10 minutes. Peel and quarter them.
3. Tear the lettuce leaves.
4. Layer the tomatoes, lettuce, cucumber, radishes, cheese, ham, and eggs in a glass bowl.
5. Serve the dressing separately. Serve with crusty French bread.

MAKES 6 TO 8 SERVINGS.

✺

Cucumber Salad

*T*his salad is good with fish, especially salmon, and boiled potatoes. Tante Lise recommends using a cheese slicer to make the cucumber slices thin.

In 1915 Thor Bjørklund invented the cheese slicer or *ostehøvel*. A poor farmer, he found it an economical way to make the cheese go around on the bread of his many children.

2 large cucumbers
6 onions, thinly sliced
⅓ cup white vinegar
5 tablespoons sugar
½ teaspoon salt
dash of pepper
chopped dill or parsley

1. Peel the cucumbers. Cut into thin slices.
2. Place in a glass bowl with onion rings.
3. Combine vinegar, 5 tablespoons water, sugar, salt, and pepper. Mix well.
4. Pour the dressing over the vegetables and toss lightly to coat evenly.
5. Cover bowl and refrigerate for several hours until the cucumbers are wilted and the flavors are well-blended.
6. Garnish with chopped dill or parsley.

MAKES 4 SERVINGS.

Cucumber salad is an excellent accompaniment to smoked salmon and hard-boiled eggs. Beer and aquavit are a must.

❧
Waffles

vafler

You'll find heart-shaped waffles on every *koldt bord* in Norway. Stores like Haram-Christensen Corp., listed at the end of the book, carry such specialty items as the vanilla sugar called for below. As a substitute, simply add a few drops of vanilla to sugar.

½ cup (1 stick) butter
2 eggs
4 tablespoons sugar
1 teaspoon vanilla sugar
2½ cups whole milk
1¾ cup all-purpose flour

1. Melt the butter. Pour it into a bowl.
2. Add eggs, sugar, vanilla sugar, milk, and flour. Beat until smooth.
3. Let stand for at least 15 minutes. Heat waffle iron according to manufacturer's instructions.
4. Spoon about 1 tablespoon of batter into waffle iron. Turn until golden brown on both sides.

Serve with sugar, jam, or sour cream.

MAKES ABOUT 10 WAFFLES.

❧
Sour Cream Waffles

2⅓ cups sour cream
3 cups all-purpose flour
1 teaspoon salt

1. Beat sour cream, 1½ cups water, flour, and salt together until smooth. (Some recommend adding 1 egg and 1 tablespoon of sugar to mixture.)
2. Heat waffle iron according to manufacturer's instructions.
3. Spoon about 1 tablespoon of batter into waffle iron. Turn until golden brown on both sides.

Serve warm or cold with sugar or jam.

MAKES ABOUT 15 WAFFLES.

In the mid-nineteenth century two students, P. C. Asbjørnsen and Jørgen Moe, began to collect Norwegian fairy tales, documenting them in a style that was as close to the original as possible. They traveled throughout Norway to gather the stories in their natural environment and capture the colloquialisms and humor found in the forests and valleys. They discovered tales in many forms: folk tales, comical tales, stories in which animals behaved much like people, and magical stories dating to pagan times. Many characters are recognizably Norwegian; all the tales depicted the king, for example, as a wealthy farmer. The publication of Norwegian Folk Tales *had quite an impact on Norwegian national consciousness. Writers like Ibsen and Bjørnson often alluded to the collection in their renowned classics.*

In the following tale we see the respect shown the womenfolk of Norway, who traditionally ran the household while the men were off farming, fishing or, in the case of the Vikings, conquering and harrying.

THE MAN WHO KEPT HOUSE

There was once a cross and peevish man who had the idea that his wife never did enough in the house. One evening he came home from the haymaking, swearing and grumbling like a bear with a sore head.

"Oh my dear, don't scold so!" said his wife. "Tomorrow we'll change jobs. I'll go out with the haymakers and you can do the housework."

The man liked this plan well enough and said he was willing.

Early next morning the wife shouldered the scythe and went out into the meadow to cut hay, and the man set about working in the house. First he thought he would churn butter, but after churning a while he felt thirsty and went down to the cellar to tap ale. While he was tapping ale into a bowl, he heard the pig wander into the house. He darted up the cellar steps with the tap in his hand to get to the pig before it could upset the churn. But when he found the churn knocked over and the pig gobbling up the cream now spilt all over floor, he flew into such a rage that he clean forgot about the barrel of ale and made a bee-line for the pig. He caught up with it in the doorway and gave it a stout kick, so that it never stirred again. Then it dawned on him that he still had the tap in his hand, but by the time he reached the cellar the barrel was dry.

He set out for the milk-shed once more and found enough cream to fill the churn and kept on churning away, for he wanted to have butter ready for dinner. After he had been churning a while, he suddenly remembered that there was a cow at home in the stable still without a thing to eat or drink at this late hour. It seemed too far to take her to the field, and he thought he might as well put her to graze on the roof, there being turf roof on the farmhouse with thick, rich grass. The house was on a steep hillside and he was sure he could get the cow up on the roof without mishap if he laid a plank across. But he did not dare let go of the churn either, for fear of it being upset by the baby who was crawling about on all fours. So he hoisted the churn on his back and went out to water the cow before he led her up to the roof. He seized a bucket to fetch water from the well. But when he bent over the side of the well to draw up the water the cream poured out of the churn and ran down his neck.

It was getting on for dinnertime, and he still had no butter. So he thought he had better make porridge and hung a pot of water over the hearth. Then it crossed his mind that the cow might fall off the roof and break her legs or her neck, and so he went up to tether her safely. He tied a loop around the cow's neck, slipped the rope down through the chimney, and tied the other end round his own leg, for the water was already boiling in the pot and he had to start mixing the porridge. While he was doing so, the cow did fall off the roof after all and pulled the man up the chimney by the leg. There he got stuck, and the cow outside was in a fine pickle, dangling beside the wall, neither up nor down.

The wife had been waiting hour after hour for the man to come and call her in to dinner, but time dragged on and nothing happened. At last she grew weary and started for home. As soon as she caught sight of the unhappy cow hanging there, she went up to it and cut the rope with her scythe. Then the man fell down the chimney, and when the wife came in he was standing on his head in the porridge pot.

—Excerpted with permission from
A Time for Trolls, Fairy Tales from Norway.

✹✹

> *That sandwiches are no more food*
> *Than love and hate are of one mood*
> *Is all I know and all I write*
> *Of love and sandwiches tonight.*
>
> —J. H. Wessel, excerpted from
> *Norway's Delight*

SMØRBRØD AND SNITTER

Everyone in Norway takes a packed lunch to work, to school, on hikes, and on ski trips. Thick slices of homemade white or dark bread spread with cheese, ham, even liver pâté are so popular that some booths around the city now sell the *Ola-pakke*, which is complete with three sandwiches, a hearty snack for Ola Nordman.

These famous Norwegian open-face sandwiches have become popular around the world. Following is a sampling of typical *smørbrød* offered in Norway. *Snitter* are bite-sized *smørbrød*.

❧
Beef Tartar

butter
4 slices white bread
1 pound ground beef
2 tablespoons chopped onion
2 tablespoons chopped beets
2 tablespoons capers
parsley
4 egg yolks, hard-boiled
salt and pepper

1. Spread butter on each piece of bread. Divide beef into four sections. Place a section on each piece of bread.
2. Garnish each serving with onion, beets, capers, and parsley. Place 1 egg yolk in the center of each piece of bread. Sprinkle with salt and pepper.

MAKES 4 SERVINGS.

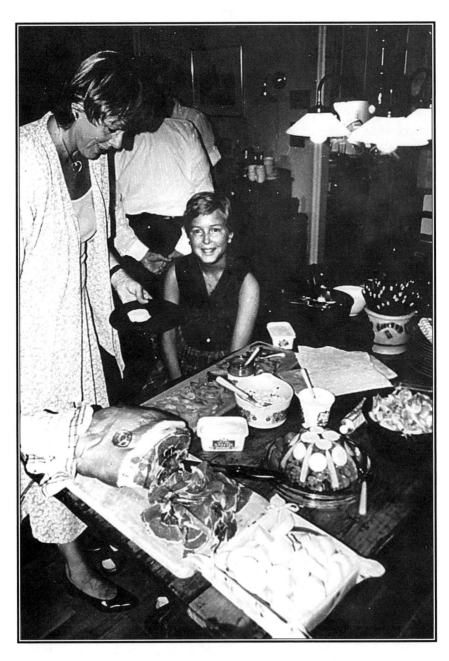

Sliced spekemat *is in the foreground. Shrimp is ready for open-faced sandwiches. Aspic is another popular addition to the* koldt bord.

🕮
Anchovy and Egg

*M*ormor often serves Norwegian anchovies with soft-boiled eggs on bread or an anchovy-and-hard-boiled-egg open-faced sandwich for lunch. Delicious! You can buy anchovies in a variety of ways in the stores of Norway. The most popular is anchovy in dill sauce.

butter
4 slices bread
4 eggs, hard-boiled or soft-boiled
8 anchovies

1. Spread butter on bread. Slice eggs.
2. Place anchovies and slices of hard-boiled egg on each piece of bread.

MAKES 4 SERVINGS.

🕮
Smoked Salmon and Scrambled Eggs

butter
4 slices bread
about 8 thin slices salmon
6 eggs, scrambled

1. Spread butter on bread.
2. Place thin slices of smoked salmon on bread. Top with scrambled eggs.

MAKES 4 SERVINGS.

🜲
Beef Cutlet Sandwich

1 onion, sliced
butter
3 or 4 beef cutlets
4 slices bread

1. Sauté onion slices in butter. Remove from pan.
2. Add beef cutlets to pan and sauté in more butter.
3. Spread butter on bread.
4. Place a beef cutlet on each slice of bread. Top with sautéed onions.

MAKES 4 SERVINGS.

🜲
Liverwurst and Beets

4 slices bread
½ cup liverwurst
about ½ cup sliced beets

1. Spread each slice of bread with liverwurst.
2. Garnish with sliced beets.

MAKES 4 SERVINGS.

✼
Cheese and Radish

4 slices bread
mustard, butter
4 slices cheese
3 radishes, sliced

1. Spread each piece of bread with mustard and butter. Place slices of cheese on bread.
2. Garnish with radish slices.

MAKES 4 SERVINGS.

✼
Cod Roe Sandwich

4 slices bread
butter
8 slices fried cod roe
½ cup mayonnaise
juice of 2 lemons

1. Spread each slice of bread with butter. Place 2 pieces of cod roe on each slice.
2. Place a dollop of mayonnaise on each piece of bread. Squeeze lemon juice over top.

MAKES 4 SERVINGS.

❧
Italian Salad with Spiced Mayonnaise

1 pound cooked, lightly salted tongue, chopped (optional)
1 pound cooked ham, chopped
1 apple, chopped
1 medium potato, boiled and chopped (optional)
1 carrot, sliced
1 tablespoon finely chopped pickles or onions
1 or 2 tablespoons finely chopped cucumber
1 cup cooked small peas or asparagus beans
spiced mayonnaise (see recipe below)
1 medium tomato, sliced
4 slices bread

MAYONNAISE

1 teaspoon mustard
1 or 2 teaspoons Worchester sauce
1 teaspoon fennel or caraway seed
¼ to ½ cup sour cream or *rømme* or ¼ cup sour cream + ¼ cup mayonnaise

1. Mix the tongue, ham, and apple together.
2. Add potato, carrot, pickles or onions, cucumber, peas or asparagus to tongue and ham mixture. Mix well.
3. Mix ingredients for the spiced mayonnaise together. Add to salad mixture. Mix well.
4. Spread Italian salad mixture on each slice of bread. Garnish with tomato slices.

MAKES 4 SERVINGS.

Jam, Juice, and Drinks

We are drinkers of Aquavit, eaters of brown whey-cheese, and guzzlers of fermented fish!

—*Pictures of Life in the Lion-Salon,* 1848

𝕏
Jam

The *Viking Cookbook* provided the following recipe as a favorite among the Vikings.

about 1 pound of raspberries or bilberries
1⅔ cups honey

1. Clean the berries. Place in pan. Cover and let simmer for about 5 minutes. Stir in honey.
2. Simmer, uncovered, over low heat for about 15 minutes. Skim the top.
3. Pour the jam into clean, hot jars. Seal each jar tightly.

Store in a cool, dark place.

MAKES TWO 8-OUNCE JARS.

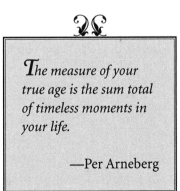

The measure of your true age is the sum total of timeless moments in your life.

—Per Arneberg

*W*ine used to be in short supply in Norway. One Norwegian bishop reputedly wrote the Pope requesting permission to use beer instead of wine for communion. His wish was not granted.

During the war, when Germans occupied my mother's home in Oslo, she and her parents, brother, and sister moved in with her grandparents. The family made wine and juice for the winter from the apples, plums, pears—indeed, from every fruit that grew in their garden. Every garden also had a rhubarb patch.

❧

Rhubarb Juice

*Y*ou can also make rhubarb juice by boiling 1½ pounds chopped rhubarb in about 8 cups of water. When the rhubarb is soft, strain the liquid and add sugar. Pour into warm bottles and cork.

4 cups chopped rhubarb
½ cup sugar

1. Mix chopped rhubarb and sugar in a saucepan and set aside for 15 or 20 minutes, or until rhubarb juice forms. Bring to a boil over medium heat, stirring constantly. Reduce heat to low and cover.
2. Let simmer until rhubarb is tender, about 15 minutes. Stir occasionally.

Set aside to cool. Refrigerate at least 2 hours before serving.

MAKES 4 SERVINGS.

"... punctually on the stroke of one, there entering the doorway was the dour and bristling presence known to all the world in caricature—caricatures which were no exaggeration, but, as in the case of Swinburne, just the man himself. The great ruff of white whisker, ferociously standing out all round his sallow, bilious face, as if dangerously charged with electricity, the immaculate silk hat, the white tie, the frock-coated martinet's figure, dressed from top to toe in old-fashioned black broadcloth, at once funereal and professorial, the trousers concertinaed, apparently with dandiacal design, at the ankles, over his highly polished boots, the carefully folded umbrella, all was there apparitionally visible before me: a forbidding, disgruntled, tight-lipped presence, starchily dignified, straight as a ramrod: there he was, with a touch, as I hinted, of grim dandyism about him, but with no touch of human kindness about his parchment skin, or small, fierce badger eyes. He might have been a Scotch elder entering the kirk. As he entered, and proceeded with precisian tread to the table reserved in perpetuity for him, and which no one else would have dreamed of occupying, a thing new and delightful—to me a mere Anglo-Saxon—suddenly happened. As one man, the whole café was on its feet in an attitude of salute, and a stranger standing near me who evidently spoke English and recognized my nationality said to me in a loud but reverent aside, "That is our great poet— Henrik Ibsen." All remained standing till he had taken his seat, as in the presence of a king ..."

—Excerpted from *The Romantic 90s*
by Richard Le Gallienne

$\mathcal{K}$arl Johansgate, Oslo's most-famous street. At precisely 1 P.M. playwright Henrik Ibsen would take his daily stroll along Karl Johansgate to the Grand Café. His statue stands outside the National Theater nearby.

The famous playwright Henrik Ibsen came to Grimstad from his birthplace of Skien to be an apothecary's assistant. He wrote his first play, *Catiline*, published in 1850, in a small room behind the shop. He left his post soon after. The pharmacy, which has been turned into the Ibsenhuset or Grimstad city museum, displays the hat, coat, and umbrella the master used for his daily stroll down to Oslo's Grand Café. *Peer Gynt* is performed in a stone quarry in Fjæreheia nearby.

Unhappy with Norway and its people, whom he thought to be narrow-minded, Ibsen and his family lived a good part of his life in Germany and Italy. When he returned to Oslo in 1891, he was welcomed as a hero. The daily stroll he took at precisely 1 P.M. from his apartment to the Grand Café on Karl Johansgata became something of a tourist attraction.

Grimstad's attractions are many. The town has one of the highest number of recorded days of sunshine of any town in Norway. Its Fuhrs wine cellar can offer you a taste of the town's own fruit wine. Grimstad also hosts the Norwegian Short Film Festival.

❧

Less good than they say for the sons of men
is the drinking oft of ale:
for the more they drink, the less can they think
and keep a watch o'er their wits.

—Håvamål, The Poetic Edda,
translated by Olive Bray,
edited by D.L. Ashliman

Norway is not only famous for its cuisine, but also for its drink—in particular for a type of spirits called *akevitt* (aquavit). Created by Eske Bille in 1531, the whisky was sent to the archbishop Olav Engelbrektsson as *Aqua Vitae,* "water of life," a cure for all ills. It was soon sold as a medicine. Old timers still swear by its health benefits, and many enjoy a small shot every night before bed.

Distilled from potatoes and made with caraway, anise, fennel, coriander, sherry, sugar, and salt, *akevitt* has actually improved considerably in taste since its creation. This progress is due to a shipowner named Jørgen Lysholm, who sent a barrel of Norwegian *akevitt* to South America for trade. No one there was interested in the liquor, however, and the barrel returned to his distillery in Trondheim. Discouraged, Lysholm opened the barrel to console himself with a drink and discovered that the long trip across the equator had improved its taste considerably. From that day on, the production of Norway's *Linie akevitt* is not complete until the liquor has been shipped in casks on a two-month round-trip to Australia. Its name refers to the fact that it passes over the equator— "the Line."

Akevitt chased with beer traditionally accompanies lutefisk, *får i kål,* and many salted and smoked dishes.

*A*kevitt *with dill and lemon. Photograph by Anne Senstad, Norwegian photographer in New York.*

*U*ntil recently 90% of Norway's population lived in rural areas. There they drank *blanda*, a mixture of water and sour whey or soured milk. A law from 1273 instructed priests to ensure people formalized their married bond with a wedding even if the parties could afford nothing but *blanda* instead of the usual beer.

Beer is still part of every Norwegian celebration. A chaser for *akevitt*, an everyday thirst-quencher on the farms, and a strong, rich drink for holidays, beer has been home brewed in Norway for more than 1000 years. The *Viking Cookbook* tells us that at most meals the Vikings served *munngodt* (good in the mouth), beer brewed from corn. Also popular was *gammelt øl*, old beer, which was *munngodt* allowed to ferment longer to produce a higher alcohol content. One ancient law stated that no one could be declared incompetent as long as he had his senses, could ride a horse, and was able to drink beer. Another stated that no agreement was legally binding until beer was served.

Even today the high price of spirits in Norway persuades many Norwegians to brew their own beer in their cellars. Beer-brewing competitions are quite popular in the countryside.

Everyone prefers beer to milk, but other drinks are considered superior even to beer—like mead and wine. Sverre's Saga tells the story of a twelfth-century Christmas banquet when the king's men drank mead in the main hall and the guests were placed in a side room and served beer. This so enraged the guests that, on the fifth day of drinking, they took up their weapons and commenced battle.

❧
Warrior's Mead

*W*hen brewing mead, make sure that your utensils and containers are as clean as possible. To brew about 32 pints of mead, you'll need a stainless steel pan that holds 44 pints, a 35-pint demijohn with a rubber seal, and a fermentation lock, plastic tubing, gauze, and a slotted ladle. The *Viking Cookbook* provided the following recipe.

6 tablespoons dried rose hips
3 tablespoons cloves
21 pints cold water
10 pints honey
1 yeast culture (see below)

YEAST CULTURE

2 cups water
2 tablespoons sugar
½ teaspoon yeast nutrient
¼ teaspoon citric acid
wine yeast for 31 pints

1. Stir rose hips and cloves into the water. Add honey until it dissolves. Simmer over low heat for about 1 hour. Continually skim the top of the water.
2. Remove from heat and set aside to cool overnight.
3. Mix ingredients for yeast culture. Bring the water and spices to a boil. Let cool overnight.
4. Reheat the honey water ("must") to lukewarm, then add the yeast culture.
5. Mix well, cover, and set aside in a warm place.
6. When the fermentation process has begun, quickly pour the must into a demijohn and seal with the fermentation lock and rubber seal.
7. Leave the must to ferment in a warm place for about a week to 10 days.
8. Strain the must and pour it back into the demijohn.

9. Seal once more and leave in a warm place until the fermentation process is completed. This will take another 3 to 5 weeks.
10. Strain the must once more time and pour into bottles that can be sealed.

MAKES 32 PINTS.

🐝
Eggedosis

Eggedosis, a favorite among children, is especially popular on the 17ᵗʰ of May, Independence Day. Adults add a dash of cognac for flavor.

2 egg yolks
1 egg white
sugar

1. Mix egg yolks and egg white. Add desired amount of sugar.

Serve alone or as a topping on fruit.

MAKES 2 SERVINGS.

The Boy and the Devil

Once there was a boy walking along a road cracking nuts. He came upon one that was worm-eaten, and just then he met the devil.

"Is it true what they say," said the boy, "that the devil can make himself as small as he will and force his way through pin-prick?"

"Yes," answered the devil.

"Let me see you creep into this nut, then," said the boy. And the devil did so.

When he had crept right in through the worm-hole, the boy pushed a twig into it. "Now I've got you," he said, and put the nut in his pocket.

Further along the road he came to a forge. There he went in and asked the smith if he would crack open the nut for him.

"Yes, that's easy enough," replied the smith. And he took his smallest hammer, placed the nut on the anvil and hit it, but it would not break. So he took a bigger hammer, but that was not heavy enough either. And he tried an even bigger one, and that was no good. Then the smith got angry, and seized his sledge-hammer. "I'll smash you if it's the last thing I do!" said he and struck with all his might. And then the nut burst into splinters with such a roaring crash that half the roof flew off and it seemed as if the whole smithy would tumble down.

"The flaming devil must have been in that nut!" said the smith.

"He was!" said the boy.

—Excerpted from *A Time for Trolls, Fairy Tales from Norway*

Fish Dishes

Yea! The fish in the seas are our daily bread,
Should we lose them, we will suffer and dread,
Forced to utter our miserable sighs.

—Petter Dass, from *Guide to the History of Lofoten*

❧

What would we do without the sea? Carry our boats?

—Old Norwegian saying from
Guide to the History of Lofoten

*T*he temperate waters of the Gulf Stream provide a favorable climate and a rich supply of plankton along the ice-free Norwegian coast. Indeed, green forests cover much of the terrain here. In summer months you might even see Norwegians sunbathing on the white beaches along the coast. And the fish abound! You can fish for more than 200 kinds of edible fish in these coastal waters.

The sea, which is called Highway 1, has served as the country's most important communications route for thousands of years—even before Leif Eriksson crossed the Atlantic to settle in North America 1,000 years ago. Before people ventured out into the open sea, the "northern way" (from which Norway got its name) served to unify otherwise isolated settlements.

Not surprisingly, three quarters of Norwegian people live along the coast. Cities like Stavanger, the chief town of Rogaland (see page 106), have been wholly dependent on the sea since the twelfth century, as is evident from archaeological excavations on display at Stavanger's Iron Age Farm in Ullenshaug. In addition to this famous archaeological museum and an oil museum, Stavanger hosts some of the best lobster in Norway and a herring factory, testament to the industry that enabled the city to survive until oil put it on the map. Norway is Europe's largest oil exporter today; oil and gas have been extracted from the Norwegian continental shelf since the 1970s.

Fish is as important a staple as ever in today's Norway. Record numbers of fish of all sizes are caught here. Fishermen have reported cod weighing as much as 37 kilograms (82 pounds), and the Norwegian record for halibut is a whopping 102 kilograms (225 pounds). Although it seems that everyone is a fisherman, state and regional regulations do monitor fishing. Fishing rights in Norwegian water usually belong to the landowner; about two-thirds of all land in Norway is privately owned. Local authorities administer fishing rights on common crown property, which is situated mainly in Nord-Trøndelag and Sør-Trøndelag. You must have a fishing license to fish and permission from the landowner to fish on his property. Fishing fees may be paid at any post office in Norway; licenses can be purchased from the landowner, at sporting goods dealerships, and at tourist information offices. If you bring a fishing rod from abroad, a local vet must disinfect it before you fish in Norway. No local license is required for seawater fishing. About 200 species of saltwater fish live and/or breed off the coast of Norway. If you are interested in fishing in Norway, read *Angling in Norway*, available from the tourist board, and contact the Directorate for Nature Management. If you visit in August, you can take part in the International Sea Fishing Festival in Stavanger.

Most popular fishing areas lie along the Atlantic Road, which connects many little islands. The fjord between Gjemnes, Bergsøy, and Torvikbukt is renowned for its trout, and the Surna river is known for salmon. The Hardangervidda, another angler paradise, is home to thousands of rivers and lakes full of mountain trout. Spend the night in one of its many *hytter* and have your catch cooked for dinner.

The following recipe is from Lierne in the county of Nord-Trøndelag.

❧
Fish in Brine

*S*alting and smoking were not the only methods by which the Norwegians preserved meat and fish. Salmon and trout were also cured under pressure in brine.

1 pound trout or char
1 tablespoon salt
1 teaspoon sugar

BRINE

4¼ cups whey
2 tablespoons salt
1 tablespoon sugar

1. Clean and rinse the fish. Pat dry.
2. Mix the salt and sugar together. Place the fish belly up in a plastic pail. Sprinkle the mixture on the fish bellies. Continue to layer fish and salt and sugar mixture. Cover with a clean cloth. Refrigerate for a week.
3. After a week, boil the whey with salt and sugar. Set aside to cool. Rinse the fish thoroughly. Place in a clean plastic pail. Cover with brine. Cover with a clean cloth. Place a light pressure on the fish and make sure that the brine covers them completely. Store in a cellar for 7 or 8 weeks.
4. Wash, skin, and fillet the fish.

Serve with boiled potatoes and flatbread and butter.

MAKES 3 OR 4 SERVINGS.

If it should be to his satisfaction, no fish shall be salted but that it is not also soured.

—Bishop Erik Pontoppidan, *This is Norway*

*W*inters are long in Norway. Because animals can only pasture for a few short summer months, Norwegians have always been dependent on dried, smoked, salted, and pickled meat and fish. Cod, for example, is especially tasty salted, dried, and aged. In winter the Norwegian arctic cod travels about 800 kilometers (500 miles) from the Barents Sea to spawn in the Vestfjord between the Lofoten Islands and the mainland. There temperatures, salinity, depth, and currents of the sea provide the perfect conditions for the *skrei,* or spawning cod. A large female can spawn up to three million eggs, which hatch in two to four weeks. During the first year only about twenty survive and develop into fish.

Two varieties of cod prepared from these fish are especially popular. *Tørrfisk* is a favorite among the old timers of Lofoten. *Torsk,* the word for cod, comes from the word "to dry." The cod is tied together in pairs and hung on racks, or *gjell,* to dry by the sun and wind. On fish-fetching day, traditionally June 12, the fish is taken down from the racks.

Tørrfisk was a significant trade asset in the old days; indeed, people still say that the fish drying on the racks smells like money. It was also an important addition to the Viking menu during their long journeys. The Henningsvær church in Lofoten nearby was even built to look like the *gjell.*

A second way to prepare the cod is to dry it on bare rocks; drying the fish close to the fjord during the dry summer months is said to add flavor. This *klippfisk* is split down the middle and the backbone removed. Sprinkle the fish liberally with salt and then set it out to dry. Its name comes from the rocks, or *klipper,* on which the fish were placed to dry. *Klippfisk* must be soaked in fresh water for a day before it is cooked. Today most are dried in thermostat-regulated drying rooms.

For centuries towns have been trading in *klippfisk* and *tørrfisk*. In 1691, for example, Dutch Jappe Ippes started the *klippfisk* trading industry in Ålesund, the fisheries capital of South Norway. He made a fortune exporting the dried product to Catholic countries where it was eaten on fast days. Kristiansund is still the major port of the *klippfisk* export trade in southern Norway.

Both *klippfisk* and *tørrfisk* will keep for years and are considered very nutritious.

🐟

Poached Klippfish

2 pounds salted, dried cod

1. Remove any remaining skin and bones from cod. Cut the fish into large pieces. Place in a pot of water.
2. Bring to a boil. Reduce heat and let simmer gently for 15 minutes.

Serve with creamed carrots, boiled potatoes or bacon, and melted butter.

MAKES 4 OR 5 SERVINGS.

Fish drying under the general store at Nusfjord.

The seaman's Memorial Hall, which was raised after World War I, was consecrated by King Håkon VII on August 1, 1926. The Memorial Hall was erected in memory of the Norwegians in the merchant fleet who lost their lives during World War I. Today it is a memorial to the Norwegian seamen who lost their lives in the two world wars.

My great grandfather was the president of Norges Skibsførerforbund and the head of the building committee. He and his fellow seamen presented the royal ship Norge to King Håkon VII on his seventy-fifth birthday. The Norge (Norway) is still the royal ship today. This picture shows him walking with King Håkon.

Vandrer som stanser her, husk sjømannens vei og mål
og hans hvile.

Husk hans vei, den er som havet, solbeskinnet,
Stormende or atter stille, men bestandig ledet av stjerner.

Husk hans mål, en havn, nær eller fjern, hvor han
Henter håp om å vende tilbake.

Husk hans hvile og hans hvilesteder:
Havet, himlen og vårt hjerte.

Som morild efter skib skinner og slukner hans vei,
Men heder og vart hjerte.

Som morild efter skib skinner og slukner hans vei,
Men heder og mot folger ham til målet, og der hvor han
hviler, velsignes hans navn.

The wanderer who stops here, remember the seamen's road and aim
and his rest.

Remember his way, it's like the ocean, sundrenched,
stormy yet quiet, but always led by the stars.

Remember his aim, his harbor, near or far away, where he
picked up hope of returning.

Remember his rest and resting place:
the ocean, the sky, and our hearts.

Like a flame after the ship shines and then fades his way,
with honor and courage follow him to the aim, and where he
rests, blessed be his name.

—Herman Wildenvey

When the *skrei* arrive in Lofoten in January, the islanders often enjoy a dish of *skreimølje,* or cod boiled with roe and liver. Vinegar, salt, whole peppercorns, bay leaves, and onion are added for taste.

Mølje, a delicacy in the Lofoten Islands, is considered very nutritious. You can thank Norwegian pharmacist Peter Møller for the cod liver oil for sale in every health food store around the world today. In 1854 Møller built a lined cauldron and steam-boiled the fresh cod livers to improve the quality of the oil. His medicinal cod liver oil, which became renowned for carrying vitamins A and D and the Omega 3 unsaturated fatty acids, received many awards at trade fairs. Cod liver oil soon became second only to stockfish as Norway's most valuable commodity. Professor Schlotz even prescribed cod liver oil in his famous Oslo breakfast, which is served at most Oslo schools to ensure that all children received a nutritious breakfast. *Norway's Delight* gives the Oslo breakfast recipe as follows:

1. 2 cups whole milk
2. 1 large piece of flatbread spread with margarine and cheese
3. wholemeal bread with cheese or liver pâté
4. 1 small tablespoon cod liver oil (from September to May)
5. one slice of raw cabbage or half an orange or one apple

Every summer thousands of barrels of cod liver oil are still exported from Norway. Today the cod livers are boiled or steamed in Å, a tiny town located at the tip of the Lofoten islands. The cod liver oil factory there displays the production equipment used in Møller's time, when the livers were left in the vats to ferment in the heat of the summer before the oil was extracted. You can buy bottles of the oil here—as well as Møller's less famous cod liver oil lamps.

❧
Poached Halibut

2 pounds halibut fillets
2 teaspoons salt per quart water
1 teaspoon whole peppercorns

1. Wash and clean the fillets. Cut into serving portions.
2. Bring a large pan of water to a boil. Add salt and peppercorns.
3. Remove from heat. Add the fillets. Return to heat. Let simmer very gently for about 15 minutes.

Serve with boiled potatoes, sour cream, and cucumber salad (see page 32).

MAKES 4 OR 5 SERVINGS.

The skrei *arrive in the Lofoten Islands in January.*

⁂

Poached Salmon

*J*ust think. The Vikings were forced to wait until the salmon swam upstream to spawn before they could go salmon fishing. Today you can enjoy salmon from Norway's many fish farms year-round.

2 salmon steaks
3 tablespoons salt
whole peppercorns
lemon, sliced thin

1. Clean the salmon. Cut about ½ inch thick and rinse well.
2. Bring a large pan of water to boil.
3. Add salt, peppercorns, and lemon.
4. Add salmon. Reduce heat and let simmer for 6 to 8 minutes. To serve cold, cook the fish for 3 minutes and allow to cool in the water.

Serve cold salmon with sour cream and a green salad. Serve hot with cucumber salad (see page 32), Sandefjord butter (page 71), and boiled potatoes.

MAKES 2 SERVINGS.

❧
Sandefjord Butter
Sandefjordsmør

Sandefjord, a delightful little coastal town, is kept busy with the ferries that sail to Strömstad in Sweden. The waterfront is lined with fishing and prawn boats selling their freshly cooked catches. Parks and gardens lead to the nineteenth-century Viking-inspired municipal baths in the center of town; today the building is a civic center. Also visit the whaling museum here, the only one of its kind in Europe.

The following recipe was passed on to my mother from her childhood friend Anne-Marie.

1 cup heavy cream
¾ cup butter, softened (1½ sticks)
chopped parsley

1. Boil cream until only half remains.
2. Add butter gradually while stirring. Be sure that cream does not come to a boil again.
3. Add parsley to taste. Sauce should be thick and creamy.

Serve with any boiled fish.

MAKES 4 SERVINGS.

Chef Anne Greta Forde of Børsen Spiseri.

While we were in the Lofoten Islands, we stopped for dinner in Svolvær at the Børsen Spiseri. There chef Anne Greta Forde served us a fabulous dinner of typical Lofoten cuisine.

Cod, perhaps the most common fish from these shores, was the main focus of our menu. Not a bit was wasted. First Anne Greta served her famous cod tongue dish. Village children make small change during the fishing season by collecting the tongues of the fresh cod on long skewers and selling them to restaurants. Anne Greta coated the tongue with a mixture of flour, salt, and pepper and fries it in butter. It was delicious. She recommends serving it in a white wine sauce. Simply remove the tongue from the pan, pour a few tablespoons of dry white wine into the pan, and mix the wine with the pan scrapings. Serve on a bed of green leafy lettuce with sunflower seeds, baby tomatoes, and baby onions. Sprinkle with olive oil and chopped spring onions. Cod tongue is also tasty with rice and watercress salad.

Next we tried cod fish eggs which had been salted, sugared, and finally smoked. They, too, were delicious. We continued with Anne Greta's specialty *bokna*, or half-dried cod, which is left to dry for two or three weeks before being cut into pieces. The cod pieces are placed under running water for 14 to 16 hours and then boiled in salted water. She poured melted butter mixed with a chopped boiled egg and bacon bits over the fish and served it with creamed carrots and boiled potatoes garnished with dill.

Finally we tasted the "fisherman's wife pan." This dish is a hodgepodge of ingredients—whatever you have in the cupboard mixed with whatever your fisherman husband catches that day. Anne Greta first sautéed chopped onion in butter, a few tablespoons dry white wine, and fish stock. She added chopped carrots, chopped leeks, and chopped asparagus. She completed the dish with red fish, catfish, salmon, and mussels, and scallops. You can make a saffron sauce by adding a few strands of saffron to the pan. Mix 1 cup white wine and about 3 cups fish stock to the pan scrapings. Pour over the dish before serving.

For dessert we ate *rabarbra*, a simple rhubarb dessert made by boiling rhubarb with sugar and potato flour (see page 230).

Following is another recipe from Anne Greta for rainbow trout, which are caught in Lake Følstra in her hometown of Skei.

❦

Rainbow Trout

½ cup all-purpose flour
1 tablespoon salt
1 tablespoon pepper
1 pound rainbow trout
butter for frying

SAUCE

1 cup crème fraîche
chives, parsley, salt, and pepper

1. Mix flour, salt, and pepper together. Coat trout in the mixture.
2. Brown fish in butter. Remove fish from pan.
3. To make sauce, add the crème fraîche to the pan scrapings. Add chives, parsley, salt, and pepper to taste. Mix well. Pour over trout.

Serve immediately with boiled fingerling potatoes and cucumber salad (see page 32).

MAKES ABOUT 3 SERVINGS.

*K*abelvåg is the oldest village in Lofoten; the first church here was built in 1120. The church pictured here, which was built in 1898, stands outside Kabelvåg and is the largest timber church north of Trondheim. It holds 1200 seats and is full during the fishing season. The Trollsteine, reputedly used as an altar when King Øystein came here in 1120, stands outside the church.

*T*he rivers of Norway are flush with salmon. The royal families of Sweden and Norway have been known to frequent the river Lærdal, which is considered the best river for salmon in the north. Lakselv in Finnmark is also renowned for its salmon fishing; *lakselv* actually means "salmon river." The Stjørdal river, which also claims some of the best salmon fishing in Norway, was visited by Victorian anglers—including George V—as early as 1858. Sea trout, red char, grayling, perch, pike, gwyniad, and freshwater herring are also abundant here. The Sørlandet island community of Lyngør boasts the river Storelva, where you can actually watch the salmon leaping up the rapids.

The largest salmon ever caught in Norway was caught by farmer and postal worker Henrik Henriksen beneath Storfossen (the Great Fall) on the River Tana. It took him nine hours to catch the fish, which weighed 35.89 kilograms (79 pounds). He was paid 1.50 kroner (about 50 cents) for the prize.

Norway also boasts the smallest salmon river in the world, which is located beside Sykkylven in southern Norway.

⅋

Butterfly Salmon

laksebutterfly

5 pounds salmon or fillets of salmon
2 to 3 tablespoons butter
juice of 1 small lemon
salt
pepper

Preheat oven to 300° F.

1. If filleting salmon, cut the fish down the middle but do not completely separate the pieces. Spread the fish open.

2. Melt the butter. Add 1¼ cups water and lemon juice to melted butter.
3. Pour the butter mixture into a shallow baking dish. Place the salmon fillets on top. Sprinkle with salt and pepper.
4. Bake for 15 to 20 minutes. After 5 or 10 minutes turn the fish.

Serve with salmon sauce (see below) or Sandefjord butter (see page 71), and asparagus or sugar peas.

MAKES 4 SERVINGS.

❦
Salmon Sauce

1 medium onion, chopped
¾ to 1 cup butter (1½ to 2 sticks)
10 fillets anchovies
1½ pounds spinach, coarsely chopped (1½ 10-ounce packages frozen spinach), adding more or less as desired

1. Bring ⅔ cups water to a boil. Add onion and let simmer until onion is soft, 3 or 4 minutes. Add butter.
2. Cut anchovies into bite-size pieces. Add to water.
3. Just before serving, add coarsely chopped spinach as desired. Serve with Butterfly Salmon.

MAKES 4 SERVINGS.

*T*he Vikings roasted fish and meat in clay pots that stood over a fire in the middle of the floor. Today we use aluminum foil.

Pollack, one of the fish that is especially good served the following way, hunts on the surface of the water in summer and is easy to catch. The largest ever caught in Norway weighed 44 pounds. You are more likely to catch a two-pounder.

❧
Fish Baked in Foil

2 pounds any fish or fish fillet (cod, pollack, trout, salmon)
butter
salt
chopped parsley, chives, or dill
1 onion, chopped
spinach, apple slices, leek (optional)

Preheat oven to 400° F.

1. Place the fish in a piece of buttered aluminum foil. Season with a little salt, parsley, chives, or dill. Add a bit of chopped onion, spinach, apple, or leek and another dab of butter.
2. Seal the foil tightly. Bake for 10 to 20 minutes.

Serve unopened on hot plates with boiled potatoes.

MAKES 4 OR 5 SERVINGS.

For a thousand years, visiting fishermen have used the Lofoten Islands as their base during the winter fishing season. At first they were forced to spend the night under their sails, under their overturned vessels, or even in caves or under rocks. Gradually, as the commercial fish trade began to develop in Svolvær and neighboring towns, residents built rorbuer or rorbu cabins to house them during the fishing season. Some reports credit King Øystein for the first rorbuer, who reputedly built the cabins in 1120 along the coast of the island of Austvågøy for income. As increasing numbers of fishermen came to take advantage of a comfortable place to stay, the total catch for the season increased as well. In turn, the king, who received a percentage of the catch, made more money. A statue of King Øystein stands in Kabelvåg.

   Today rorbuer are still popular places to stay. They are usually two-room cabins, with the fisherman using one room for living quarters and the other to store his nets, food, and bait supplies. Some of the original rorbuer have now been restored for tourists.

❧
Salmon Roll

4 large or 8 small white or green asparagus
1 pound salmon, skinned and boned
1 bunch parsley, chopped
juice of 1 lemon
salt
ground white pepper

BUTTER SAUCE

1 shallot, minced
½ cup dry white wine
¼ cup heavy cream
1¾ sticks butter

1. Steam the asparagus. Set aside to cool.
2. Cut the salmon fillet into 4 thin slices.
3. Lay one slice of salmon on a flat surface. The kitchen counter works well.
4. Place 1 or 2 stalks of the cooled asparagus in the center of the slice. Season with parsley, lemon juice, salt, and white pepper. Roll the salmon around the asparagus. Repeat with remaining salmon slices.
5. Steam the salmon rolls for 3 to 4 minutes.
6. To make the sauce, sauté the shallot in the white wine until the liquid is reduced to 1 tablespoon.
7. Add the cream. Bring almost to a boil.
8. Cut the butter into small pieces and add little by little while stirring. Do not allow to boil. You may prepare your sauce ahead of time and reheat it over boiling water. Remove the shallot before serving if desired.

MAKES 4 SERVINGS.

*M*y mother's father was born in Larvik, a charming seaside resort town situated in Vestfold between Lake Farris, famous for its mineral waters, and Larvikfjord. Larvik developed as a whaling station and ship building center; the ship *Fram* was built here. Timber and timber exporting are now the town's main industries.

The birthplace of Thor Heyerdahl, Larvik also boasts a seafaring museum that houses Heyerdahl's vessels *Kon Tiki* and *Ra*. Also worth seeing are Larvik's churches and the war memorial created by Gustav Vigeland. My grandfather was baptized in the twelfth-century Tjølling church; its Rococo baptismal font is unusual for Norway.

My mother spent her summers in Larvik's neighboring town of Ula. An archipelago popular for its beaches and bathing, Ula is also known for its Ulabrand statue. It faces the sea as if waiting for the boats from Holland that came carrying pipes and bulbs to these shores centuries ago.

*T*hor Heyerdahl and tante Lise at the Kon Tiki Museum in Oslo. The famous navigator still spends his time exploring. Legend has it he didn't even have to fish while on his balsa raft. The flying fish just flew right into his sleeping bag at night!

🌾

If any people in the world owns its land with honor and right, has conquered it, not from other people, but in obedience to the Creator's stern commandment that man shall eat his bread in the sweat of his brow, it is we Norwegians, who call Norway our country.

—Sigrid Undset, *Return to the Future,*
excerpted from *A History of Norway*

*F*ried fish is especially good when accompanied by mixed Norwegian vegetables. Thanks to the Gulf Stream, farmers can grow a variety of vegetables that can be stored throughout the year, including carrots, onions, cabbage, and rutabaga, also known as "Nordic oranges." What Henrik Ibsen called the "quiet war of the farmer" resulted in a countryside rich with succulent vegetables.

To make a tasty vegetable side dish, simply brown diced carrots, rutabaga, celery root, parsley root, parsnip, and leek in a little oil or butter. Sprinkle with chopped parsley before serving.

❧
Grilled Salmon

BUTTER SAUCE

¼ cup butter
crushed juniper berries
3 tablespoons chopped chives

4 salmon steaks
1 or 2 tablespoons butter for grilling or frying
1 teaspoon salt

1. Mix the ingredients for the butter sauce. Refrigerate.
2. Grill the salmon in butter for about 3 minutes per side. Sprinkle salt on both sides.
3. Serve with the butter sauce and boiled vegetables.

MAKES 4 SERVINGS.

The thirty-five people who reside in the beautiful Lofoten town of Nusfjord enjoy the quiet wintertime. In summer the rorbuer *here are overflowing with fishermen. Unlike many* rorbuer *built in response to the increasing numbers of tourists arriving at the islands, these rental cottages are the real thing. The word* rorbu *comes from* ror, *"to row," and* bu, *"dwelling." Old timers still ask if one is to "row [fish] this season." Rent at the Nusfjord* rorbuer *even includes a row boat.*

Nusfjord was put under a preservation order in 1975, and today it is the best-preserved fishing village in Norway. Be sure to stop in at the general store for a cup of coffee and a chat with Inger-Lise, the proprietor.

*N*othing beats prawn suppers, prawns piled high on crusty white bread spread with butter and topped with mayonnaise and lemon. It is a favorite during the summer in Norway. It also makes a delicious *smørbrød* and tastes heavenly under the country's white nights.

Norway's summer sun shines on the north of the country for 24 hours a day and gives Norway more hours of light in summer than any other country. Norwegians don't want to miss a second of it. City streets are as busy at 2 A.M. as they are at 2 P.M. Visitors with small children call on their friends in the middle of the night. People play golf, dine, and swim under the white nights. Little sleep is needed during these few months. Norwegians sleep in winter. Summers are spent outdoors and on—or in—the fjords, and some of my best memories are the weeks-long sailing trips I took with my cousins along the coast of southern Norway. One trip took us to scenic Verdens Ende, "the World's End," about 30 minutes' drive from Tønsberg at the southernmost tip of the southernmost island Tjøme. These rock-covered beaches were named centuries ago by visiting Victorians.

Most fun, however, were the trips taken on Midsummer Night's Eve or *St. Hans Aften*, the longest night of the year June 21. Bonfires light up the coastline in celebration of the pagan festival of *solsnu*, the turn of the sun. Boats tie alongside each other so thick that you can literally stroll deck by deck across wide fjords from shore to shore. Birch tree branches decorate the flagpoles, and flags wave merrily from every porch and stern. Children parade through town in national costume. Everyone stays up all night to witness the longest day of the year. The Trondheim golf course, the most northerly in the world, even hosts a Midnight Golf Tournament played from 11 P.M. until 2 A.M.

Within the Arctic Circle itself, Midsummer Night's Eve is the one night of the year when the sun never makes it below the horizon. The only town actually situated inside the arctic climate zone is Vardø, Norway's most easterly town. With its barren landscape Vardø was perhaps not surprisingly regarded as the realm of the devil. In the seventeenth century Vardø was the site of Norway's largest witch hunt; more than eighty women were burned alive there.

🎜

Shrimp Supper

1 loaf white bread, sliced
½ cup (1 stick) butter
3 pounds fresh baby shrimp
½ cup mayonnaise
3 lemons
dill

1. Spread a thick slice of white bread with butter. Peel shrimp and pile high on the bread.
2. Add a dollop of mayonnaise. Squeeze lemon juice on it and garnish with dill. Repeat for remaining slices.

Makes 6 servings.

❧

Fola, fola, Blakken!
Nå er Blakken god og trett;
Blakken skal bli god og mett.
Å, fola, fola, Blakken!

*H*orse Blakken!
Now is Blakken good and tired;
Blakken shall be good and full.
Horse, horse, Blakken.

Tønsberg, founded by King Harald Haarfagre in the ninth century, is considered the oldest town in Norway; the chronicler Snorre recorded that the town existed even before Haarfagre arrived. Located about 100 kilometers (62 miles) from Oslo on the Oslofjord, it had a reputation as a safe harbor and a good place to settle. In the Middle Ages Tønsberg became a major trading center. Unfortunately only the renovated Tønsberg Brygge by the waterfront is reminiscent of that time.

Many believe that this nursery rhyme, which was sung by Queen Blanka to her baby son, originated in Tønsberg. She arrived here in 1335 to marry the 18-year-old King Magnus Eriksson.

> *Had I known it was so beautiful here, I would have come before.*
>
> —Bjørnstjerne Bjørnson speaking of Hardanger

Norway is the northernmost country in the world in which apples can grow, and most are found in Hardanger. English monks brought the first seeds to Lofthus in the twelfth century and planted them at the Cistercian monastery, at that time located on the present-day Opedal farm (see page 197). The monks can also claim the well-known "Monksteps," *Munketrappene*, that wind their way up the mountainside behind Lofthus. In order to ease access to the Hardangervidda Plateau, the monks carved out huge blocks of stone, which they transported up the mountainside to make the 616 steps. The monastery was closed after the Lutheran reformation arrived around 1537, and only *Munketrappene* remain.

In addition to apple seeds, the monks brought their taste for apple cider, quickly a favorite among the Norwegians as well. During blossom time in May, farmers pick the more than 600,000 fruit trees in Hardanger to make traditional Hardanger apple cider.

Salmon Marinated in Hardanger Apple Cider

¾ pound salmon
½ cup apple cider
1 teaspoon parsley
1 teaspoon chives
1 teaspoon dill
salt
sugar
freshly ground pepper

1. Clean the salmon and remove skin and bones. Cut into very thin slices and place in a dish with a raised edge.
2. Mix the cider, parsley, chives, and dill in a food processor.
3. Sift salt, sugar, and pepper over the salmon. Use slightly more sugar than salt.
4. Pour the cider and herb mixture over the salmon.
5. Refrigerate for about 3 hours.

Good as an appetizer. Serve with sour cream or crème fraîche mixed with some of the marinade. Or serve as a main dish with fresh lettuce leaves and caviar.

MAKES 4 SERVINGS.

In the nineteenth century you could find a kjenga, *or drinking bowl, on every farm in Hardanger. Important events were celebrated with a bowl of ale from the house barrel. The ale was carried from the cellar in* kjenger *and passed around the table. A slight depression was built into tables to gather any drops that spilled out of the bowl.*

❧

I'm not from Norway—I'm from Bergen.

*T*hey say that Norwegians are born with skis. "A hard delivery," admits tante Lise on the tours she takes around Norway. "But imagine living in Bergen, where they are born with an umbrella as well!"

Olav Kyrre ("the Peaceful"), who ruled Norway between 1066 and 1093, is credited with founding the beautiful city of Bergen in 1070. A trade hub for merchants, it was the most important town in medieval Norway, the country's capital in the 1200s, and the largest city in Norway for 600 more years. Bergen was also a Hanseatic League port in the fourteenth century.

The capital of fjords, Bergen is within reach of some of Norway's most beautiful, including the Sognefjord, the longest in the world and home to five of Norway's famous stave churches, the Nordfjord, and the gorgeous Geirangerfjord, best seen on a summer dance cruise. For a spectacular view of the city and its fjords, take the funicular up Mount Fløyen or Mount Ulriken, the highest of its seven mountains.

Bergen is close to some of Norway's most beautiful fjords, including the Geirangerfjord. The word "fjord" or "fiord" is one of Norwegian's contributions to the English language.

Although the weather in Bergen is infamous, its fish market is indeed famous. The market has operated for centuries alongside the many sailboats in the Bergen harbor. It is a favorite among Bergen housewives, tourists, and fishermen in the mood for prawns, crab claws, herring, as well as fruit and vegetables. The other most famous attraction of Bergen is Bryggen, a collection of medieval wooden houses that were once the property of the Hanseatic League. In the buildings of the Bryggen, which are on the UNESCO World Heritage List, you can visit workshops, art galleries, and weaving studios to watch craftsmen at work. Bryggen's Museum, housed in a twelfth-century building, is worth a visit. Also stop in at the twelfth-century Fana Church for an evening of traditional folk tunes and at the Norges Fiskerimuseum for information about the country's fishing industry. You'll even find a Lepramuseet in Bergen. Housed in a hospital used in the Middle Ages for lepers, the museum tells of the fight against leprosy, which appeared in Viking times; Norwegian Gerhard Armauer Hansen identified the cause of leprosy, which is also called "Hansen's disease," in 1869.

❧

*O*utside Bergen, Troldhaugen ("the Hill of the Trolls") is home of Norway's most famous composer Edvard Grieg, who wrote such works as The String Quartet in G minor, opus 27, and The Mountain Troll, opus 32. He was born in Bergen in 1843 to a salt-fish merchant. "I am sure that my music has the taste of codfish in it," he once said. His grand piano still stands in the salon in the home where he lived with his soprano wife Nina for 22 years. Here he would play while she stood at his side to sing. The house is today a museum and a concert hall.

Although the Griegs lived in Bergen, many of Edvard Grieg's most famous works were written in Hardanger, where they went on holiday. While in Hardanger, the Griegs lived the Ullensvang hotel. He also built a cabin nearby where he could compose his music undisturbed. The cabin held only the piano and a stove. If Grieg discovered a listener, he would immediately stop playing. He later sold the cabin for 160 kroner cash. It stands in the garden of the Ullensvang hotel today (see page 197).

*T*roldhaugen *("the Hill of the Trolls"), Edvard Grieg's home.*

❧
Fish Cakes

1½ pounds coalfish or haddock, skinned and boiled
2 tablespoons salt
⅛ teaspoons pepper
1 tablespoon finely chopped onion
1 teaspoon cornstarch
1 tablespoon all-purpose flour
⅓ cup cream
unsalted butter

1. Grind fish with salt, pepper, chives, and the flours in a food processor.
2. Add milk while processing. Blend until smooth.
3. Form into 8 equal patties.
4. Sauté each fish cake in butter until golden brown.

Serve with boiled potatoes, fried onion, and a green salad.

MAKES 5 OR 6 SERVINGS.

Fresh fish cakes for sale.

*F*or more than a thousand years the Norwegians on the northernmost coast of Norway have been drying cod and trading it to other European countries for wine, wheat, and honey. Indeed, historians say that cod comprised about 80% of total Norwegian exports through the 1300s.

In addition to the *klippfisk* and *tørrfisk* mentioned earlier, Nordmen greatly enjoy *stokkfisk*, which is cod dried on *stokker*, or sticks. They pound the stockfish or *stoccafisso* with a wooden hammer, soak it in water, and add wood ash lye to make it soft and flavorful. In the old days birch tree ashes were used to make the lye. Today they use caustic soda and boiling water (roughly 3 tablespoons soda to each 50 pints water). After mixing the two ingredients, cool the lye and pour it over the fish. Leave it for two or three days depending on how loose you like the fish. The longer it soaks, the looser it will become. Unique to Lofoten, stockfish can only be produced where the air is the right temperature: cold enough to avoid flies and maggots but warm enough to avoid freezing.

Traditionally eaten with mustard or dipped in butter, *lutefisk*, or lye fish, is still one of Norway's most popular dishes, especially at Christmas. I've heard that the small coastal town of Drøbak near Oslo even has a *lutefisk* museum. Visitors, too, grow fond of the unique taste of stockfish. The Italian merchant Pietro Querini, for example, recorded a trip home from Lofoten in 1432 with "sixty stockfish dried in the wind, and three large loaves of rye bread, as round as we were."

𝕏

Lye Fish

lutefisk

6 pounds lye fish
2 or 3 tablespoons salt

Preheat oven to 400° F.

1. Soak fish well in water to remove the lye. Norwegians strongly recommend soaking it in running water for at least two or three days. The fish is ready when you can press a finger through a medium-size fillet without resistance.
2. Place the fish in a shallow baking dish, skin side down. Sprinkle with salt.
3. Cover with a lid or foil. Bake for about 40 minutes. You may also place the fish in a cold steel pan, salt it, and let stand for 10 minutes. Bring water to a boil. Place the fish in water and let simmer over low heat for 10 minutes.

Serve immediately with crispy bacon and bacon fat, *pinnekjøtt* "mutton ribs" (see page 129), boiled potatoes, or creamed peas (see page 145). Especially tasty with beer and aquavit. Place salt, pepper, and mustard on the table. In the north they often pour syrup and grated *geitost* over the fish.

MAKES 4 SERVINGS.

✷✷

Here! Shout the mighty falls,
Surging blindly
Between the rocks,
Anything can happen here!

—Olav H. Hauge

*O*n our way home from my family's *hytte* (vacation cottage) one day, we passed within sight of the Hardangervidda, the largest mountain plateau in Europe and 1239 meters (4065 feet) above sea level. Its landscape is varied, with deep valleys, beautiful waterfalls, and glaciers in the west in sharp contrast to its gentler eastern side. An abundance of wildlife—from 10,000 to 20,000 reindeer—lives on the plateau, and you'll find plenty of good hunting here.

The spiderweb of trails on the plateau, which were created by the first reindeer hunters, were once vital east-west communications and the only means of access to the villages in the area. Today they are well marked for hikers. If you plan a long hike, I recommend you spend the night in one of the *hytter* scattered around the plateau. Most are located about a day trip away from each other. Designed like typical Norwegian holidays homes, these cabins are built to cater to hikers. Most of the two- or four-bedroom *hytter* have electric heating, hot water, and showers. The staffed *hytter* offer typical Norwegian mountain fare like venison and mountain trout. Staff also provide packed lunches for a hike the next day. The Norwegian Touring Association is a good resource when planning a hike in the area.

One third of the Hardangervidda is protected land, including the 9,000-year-old Hardangerjøkulen glacier. It peaks at 1850 meters (6070 feet) and moves at an estimated 2 or 3 meters (7 to 10 feet) a day. Glacier walking is a popular pastime in Norway. I recommend that you take the course in glacier climbing organized by the Norwegian Touring Association. Demmevasshytta is its base camp. Climb with a guide, who can point out shades of blue and green made from the varying amounts of oxygen in the ice. The Association has an experienced glacier guide at the resort town of Finse, a popular starting point for walks on Hardangerjøkulen and the locale of the famous opening ice scene in *The Empire Strikes Back*. Other glaciers popular for climbs in Norway include the blue Jostadalsbreen; at 475 square kilometers (183 square miles), it is the largest glacier in Europe and second largest in the world. Its 26 arms stretch down the mountainsides and can grow by up to 100 meters (328 feet) every year. The ride up to the Briksdalbreen, an arm of the glacier, in a horse-drawn wagon is a popular excursion.

Most of the waterfalls, rivers, and lakes situated around the protected areas of the plateau have been converted into hydroelectric power, which has proved quite effective in Norway. (Industries and private homes obtain all their electricity from hydroelectric power; its generation represents the main source of income for many regions today, including areas like Sirdal in Sørlandet.) Vøringfossen, Norway's most famous waterfall, for example, is used for hydroelectric power. To keep the scenery beautiful and maintain water flow, Vøringfossen is "turned on" from June 1 to September 15. Even the Sysen Dam, a 1,155-meter-long (3800-foot), 84-meter-high (276-foot) hydroelectric operation, has also become a tourist attraction. We too stopped for a look one bright Saturday. The Sima Power Station is open to anyone who wants to ogle its four generators, which produce enough electricity for a town of 130,000 people. Overlooking the power station and dam is the farm Kjeåsen, located on a 600-meter-high (1968-foot) cliff and known throughout Norway as the most inaccessible farm in the world. Until a road up to it was built during the construction of the power plant, it was only accessible by a steep and dangerous path up the mountainside.

Other well-thought-out measures like the stocking of rivers and lakes are regularly taken to ensure that the area thrives in spite of hydroelectric development. In some rivers fishing has actually improved.

ᴥ
Fried Mackerel

*Y*ou can use mountain char, sea char, herring, trout, or cod for this dish.

4 mackerel
3 or 4 tablespoons all-purpose flour
1 tablespoon salt
1 teaspoon pepper
butter for browning
¾ cup sour cream
1 tablespoon chopped parsley or chives

1. Clean and dry fish. Do not remove the head and tail.
2. Mix flour, salt, and pepper. Coat fish in the mixture.
3. Brown the fish over high heat in butter.
4. Bring ¾ cup water to a boil. Pour the boiling water and the sour cream in the pan over the fish.
5. Let fish simmer until completely cooked, 7 or 8 minutes.
6. Garnish with the parsley or chives.

   Serve with fried mushrooms and boiled potatoes.

MAKES 4 SERVINGS.

*T*he southern region of Sørlandet is home to Mandal, Norway's southernmost town with a 250-acre wildlife park and well-preserved wooden houses. Centuries ago Mandal salmon was considered one of the country's great delicacies; it was so important to the town's economy that a *glade laks*, or merry salmon, was even depicted on its coat of arms. The river Audna nearby is renowned for its trout fishing; fishing for the disabled is provided beside the Gislefoss waterfall, near Audenedal.

💮

Grilled Trout

1 (6-ounce) trout with skin
salt, pepper

1. Rub the fish with salt and pepper.
2. Grill 2 or 3 minutes on each side.
3. Wrap the fish in foil and set aside for about 5 minutes before serving.

Serve with boiled potatoes and vegetables.

MAKES 1 SERVING.

*W*hat can you own when life itself is on loan!

—Arnulf Øverland

*B*aked salmon is a long-standing favorite in Norway. Indeed, when Liv Arnesen arrived at the South Pole 1994, becoming the first woman to travel solo there, she cooked Norwegian fish soup and baked salmon for the personnel at the American Amundsen-Scott Base.

It was Roald Amundsen who first arrived at the South Pole. During a sailing trip through the North-West passage from 1903 to 1906, Amundsen had mapped the magnetic North Pole and studied the Netsilik Eskimos. In 1910 he set his sights on the South Pole and set off for the Antarctic aboard the *Fram* ("Forward"), Fridtjof Nansen's old ship, now on view in Oslo. In the spring he left the *Fram* with four men and several dog sleigh teams. They reached the South Pole in late 1911. He had traveled 3,000 kilometers (1860 miles) and became the first man to reach the Pole on skis.

⅋

Baked Salmon

2 pounds salmon, filleted and boned
salt and pepper
2 tablespoons butter
1 bunch dill
juice of 1 lemon
½ cup sour cream

Preheat oven to 375° F.

1. Rub the fish with the salt and pepper. Dab the butter on the fish. Sprinkle dill over the fish.
2. Wrap each fillet in foil. Bake for 20 minutes.

Serve with lemon juice and a dollop of sour cream. Delicious with a vegetable side dish of carrots, celery, and leeks.

MAKES 6 SERVINGS.

*M*y mormor makes *fiskeboller* every time I go to Norway. *Fiskeboller* and *fiskepudding* are staples in the diet of every Nordman. Today you can buy them ready-made in any store in Norway. *Fiskeboller* are made from the same ingredients as *fiskepudding:* ground fish, flour, milk and/or cream, and spices.

❧

Fish Balls

fiskeboller

*I*f you prefer to buy fish pudding at the market and slice it for *fiskeboller,* make a simple white sauce with butter, flour, milk, and a bouillon cube.

1 pound fillet of coalfish or haddock, ground
2 teaspoons salt
1½ cups cold whole milk
1 teaspoon cornstarch
¼ teaspoon mace
parsley, chives, thyme, basil, and tarragon
1 medium onion, chopped (optional)
1 leek, chopped (optional)
2 cups cold fish stock

1. Mix ground fish and salt well. Place in a food processor and grind.
2. Add milk gradually while mixing.
3. Add cornstarch, mace, parsley, chives, thyme, basil and tarragon. Add onion and leeks if desired.
4. Form balls about the size of golf balls.
5. Bring the fish stock to a boil. Add fish balls and let simmer for 5 to 10 minutes.

MAKES 4 SERVINGS.

Every season, those waiting on land watched the boats come in. If boats were heavy, people were euphoric: "The cod has arrived!" You can get a taste of what lies below the seas around the Lofoten Islands at its aquarium in Kabelvåg. With its collection of Nordland boats and old fishermen's cabins, the regional museum of Lofoten is also worth a visit.

*T*he coastal communities of Florø, Askvoll, and Naustdal are the westernmost settlements of Norway. Several times a year Florø boasts a gigantic herring *smørgåsbord*, when a 1000-foot table groans with herring dishes to serve about 8000 hungry people. The recipe for one of the dishes is given below. The herring salting house on Store Batalden Island nearby has been converted into an art gallery.

❧
Pickled Salt Herring
innlagt sild

*T*his dish is best if made several days to a month before serving.

1 large salt herring fillet (about 1 pound)
½ cup white vinegar
¼ cup sugar
2 tablespoons chopped onion
6 white peppercorns, crushed
6 whole allspice, crushed

1. Soak herring overnight in cold water.
2. The next day, bone and/or skin the herring. Cut fish into bite-size pieces and place in a shallow dish.
3. Mix the vinegar, sugar, onion, peppercorns, and allspice with 2 tablespoons water. Pour over fish. Cover and refrigerate for at least 48 hours or until ready to serve.

MAKES ABOUT 4 SERVINGS.

Southwestern Rogaland is one of Norway's most beautiful regions. Fishing huts nestle under the Jøssingfjord rock here. The remote island of the Utsira numbers more bird species than it does people. The North Sea Road takes you past pretty villages, long sandy beaches, and fertile fields from seventeenth-century Kristiansand, founded by Christian IV to strengthen his coastal defenses, to the festival town of Haugesund. In Rogaland the charming little fishing village of Skudeneshavn, which recently won a prize in Norway's "Best-Preserved Village" competition, reflects life 150 years ago. The twelfth-century St. Olav's Church in Avaldsnes boasts the *Jomfru Marias synål*, Virgin Mary's Needle, a 20-foot-tall stone monument which leans towards the church. It is said that if the stone ever makes contact with the church wall, the Day of Judgment is at hand. Rogaland is also important as the site of the battle of Hafrsfjord around A.D. 900, which united all of Norway.

As in many parts of Norway, the towns and villages along the coast in Rogaland are inseparably linked with the sea, whether by the once-prosperous herring industry or more recently by oil and ship-building. Haugesund even hosts the August *Sildajazz* (herring jazz) festival during which its pedestrian street offers the world's longest herring buffet. The town's Dokken Museum exhibits working life in the nineteenth century during the heyday of the herring era. Harald the Fairhaired, the first ruler of Norway, is buried in Haugesund. A 17-meter (56-foot)-tall obelisk, surrounded by 29 stones, one for each of Norway's districts at the time, stands at the site. A national monument today, it symbolizes the unity of the country. Haugesund claims one other famous name; a local baker who emigrated to America had a daughter named Marilyn Monroe.

Norway's Delight provided the following recipe.

✃
Haugesund Herring

2 large pickled herrings
2 tablespoons vinegar
2 tablespoons oil
1 teaspoon pepper
3 tablespoons sugar
1 beet, finely chopped
parsley, chopped
1 onion, finely chopped

1. Soak herrings overnight or at least 12 hours. Cut into 1-inch-long pieces. Place in a flat dish with pieces close together.
2. Mix vinegar, oil, pepper, and sugar. Pour over herring.
3. Set aside for 3 hours.
4. Garnish with chopped beets, parsley, and chopped onion.

Serve with boiled potatoes and sour cream.

MAKES 4 SERVINGS.

ℜ
Herring Burgers

1½ pounds herring
2 medium boiled potatoes
¾ teaspoon salt
2¼ teaspoons potato flour (or cornstarch)
2½ cups fish stock
lard for frying

1. Clean, fillet, rinse, and dry the herring.
2. Grind in a food processor. Grind a second time with the potatoes.
3. Add salt and potato flour. Mix well. Add the fish stock. Mix.
4. Shape into round cakes. Fry in lard.

Serve with fried onion, melted butter, and boiled vegetables.

MAKES 4 SERVINGS.

*T*akk lukka varleg, ho vender seg snarleg.
Be careful with your luck. She may turn on you.

Meat Dishes

Fish is fish, but meat is food.

*D*uring Norway's two-week autumn elk hunting season, more than 8,000 elk are shot. Some weigh as much as 600 pounds. Norwegians have been hunting elk even before the Viking age. In the Iron Age hunters in the Hardanger plateau and Jotunheim covered deep pits with branches and moss into which elk and reindeer plunged headlong.

My cousin Hans Jacob went hunting for elk for the first time last year in the Odalen Valley (see side story). The small grocery store near his camp agreed to skin the elk for him, and he took it home to freeze for the recipe below and other dishes delicious in cold weather. If you're interested in seeing the elk in nature, join an elk safari in Sørlandet, Norway's southern region. Songdalen here has the largest concentration of elk in Norway.

The most famous elk ever to be hunted in Norway is memorialized in a statue in Røros in Sør-Trøndelag. A copper mining community since 1644, Røros was a struggling village before the elk, which was being hunted by a local farmer, kicked up the dirt that revealed copper. A statue of the farmer also stands nearby. Two years later, the town's first smelting works began operating; today it is a museum and exhibition building. Although none of the mines are still in operation, one has been preserved and made accessible for visitors. In addition, you can read about life in the mines in the works of Røros' famous son Johan Falkberget (1879–1967), who published his first story at age 14.

February Market is the main event in Røros each year. So many hunters and trappers met here that a royal decree in 1853 declared that from that year forward, "There shall be held in Røros a Market, which is to begin on the last but one Tuesday in the month of February and which shall continue until the following Friday." The year 2000 saw its 147th Market. You can eat, drink, and be merry here—and buy everything from animal hides to electronic equipment.

In addition to paying a visit to the Røros mines and market, I highly recommend you visit in winter and take a sleigh ride. One December my onkel Bjørn took us on an unforgettable horse-drawn sleigh ride by torchlight to celebrate my parents' 25th wedding anniversary. There's nothing quite like flying across the snow and icy lakes while snuggling up under stacks of bearskin blankets. The hiss of the runners echoes in the frozen forest. If you prefer, dog sledding is also popular in the area—as is *spark* riding. Shaped like a chair, the *spark* (which means "kick" in Norwegian) has two long flexible runners. You travel across the snow by placing one foot on a runner and the other on the road to kick yourself along. You can rent a dog sled or arrange a sleigh ride at the tourist information center in town; a *spark* is available for free.

❧❧

Herb-cured Fillet of Elk

1 tablespoon sugar
1 tablespoon salt
1 teaspoon coarsely ground pepper
1 teaspoon thyme
1 teaspoon crushed rosemary
½ cup red wine
¼ cup olive oil
2 pounds fillet of elk, cooked (substitute: beef)
lettuce leaves, onion rings, pickled cucumbers

SAUCE (OPTIONAL)

½ cup sour cream
½ cup cranberry jam (or crushed cranberries with sugar)

1. Mix the sugar, salt, pepper, thyme, and rosemary with the red wine and oil.
2. Place the fillets in a plastic bag and cover with the marinade.
3. Close the bag and refrigerate for 3 days. Turn the bag over every morning and evening.
4. Before serving, cut the meat into very thin slices. Arrange on a dish with lettuce leaves, onion rings, and pickled cucumbers. Let the dish stand at room temperature for several hours before serving.
5. Mix sour cream and cranberry jam or crushed cranberries with sugar.

Serve over elk or serve with a sweet mustard sauce.

MAKES 4 TO 6 SERVINGS.

Røros' perfectly preserved wooden houses escaped the fires that destroyed other wooden towns in old Norway. Today Røros is listed as an UNESCO World Heritage site.

A note on elk hunting in Odalen from Hans Jacob Lugg.
1½ hours drive north of Oslo

Four days in the woods with some guys from Oslo and a bunch of locals. I was really excited. This should give me an opportunity to see (or hear) Elk for my first time.

Rising 5:45 A.M. the first morning, we were ready as the light started to approach the day. I was posted near a dirt road, surrounded with trees, with views in two directions. There I sat, thinking about life, with my new rifle on my lap. The rain was drizzling and the temperature not very comfortable.

After one hour one of the locals, walking around with his elkdog, said over the radio: "Watch out guys, Elk is coming in your direction."

Suddenly she stood there watching me in the middle of the road, 150 feet away.

My heart started pounding as I aimed and pulled the trigger. BANG!

One second and the Elk was gone. It disappeared between the trees. I was afraid I had missed, or even worse, hurt the animal.

After two minutes the dog came crossing the road. We found the Elk lying 80 feet from the road. A 2½ year old female weighing about 250 kg.

This was a great moment for me. Hunting with all these experienced hunters, and I shot the first one. . . .

After four days of hunting the team had got seven Elks. I got two of them. We had lots of fresh air and many quiet hours to think about things in life.

After filling my freezer with meat I started to think how to make food out of this. Here's one suggestion:

Roasted Elk

5½ pound elk steak (leg)
salt and pepper
butter

SAUCE

4 to 5 tablespoons wheat flour
¾ cup cream
blackcurrant jelly

1. Clean the steak. Rub with salt and pepper. Dab with butter.
2. Place the steak on a grate over a pan in the oven for 1 to 1½ hours at 350° F. Check temperature with thermometer. Set aside.
3. Add water to the pan. Bring to a boil to make stock. Make gravy by mixing stock, wheat flour, cream, and blackcurrant jelly.

Serve with potatoes, rowanberry jelly, and fresh fried chanterelles.

MAKES 6 TO 8 SERVINGS.

> *O*ne doesn't paint
> after nature—
> one takes from it
> or scoops out of its
> rich vat
>
> —Excerpted from *Open City*, translated from
> Edvard Munch's diary by Gill Holland

*T*he national dish *får i kål,* or lamb in cabbage, has been a favorite for centuries. One rainy summer day during a visit to my aunt and uncle's *hytte* in Hardanger, onkel Johnny taught me the fine art of making *får i kål.* His recipe follows.

Although fishing has always been the most important source of livelihood in Norway, Norwegians of the Old Iron Age became increasingly dependent on their farms. Because the land close to the farms did not provide enough food to feed the flocks, and artificial seeding had not yet arrived, the farmer of Norway's interior regions looked to the mountains to provide pasturelands. It became obligatory to drive the cattle up into the mountains every spring; no animals were allowed to stay home and use up the winter supplies. Indeed, supplies were so scarce that often the cattle had to be carried out of the barns in spring.

It soon became the custom for the women of farm families to live in the mountains all summer. Every farm had a *seter,* or group of cabins, where the women tended the cattle and sheep and made enough butter and cheese to last through the winter. These days most *seter* have become traditional holiday homes or *hytter.*

Like my aunt and uncle, many modern Norwegians, who adore their country and are great sport and nature enthusiasts, own a *hytte* somewhere in the country. Seven out of ten Norwegians vacation in Norway. One holiday cabin in my family is a traditional, grass-roofed, cozy place with a view of three waterfalls and the majestic Hardanger glacier Jøkul. Another is in southern Norway perched on the edge of a fjord. *Hytter* are not only summer homes. Norwegians are not afraid of winter, and even though they can only reach it by ski or by foot, my aunt and uncle enjoy their *hytte* as much in winter as they do in summer.

If you don't own a cabin, you can rent one any time of year through Den Norske Hytteformidling and Fjordhytter Den Norske Hytteformidling (see Contacts on page 277). If you prefer camping, you're in good company. Norwegian law actually encourages you to enjoy the country's beautiful landscape: "The right of passage on uncultivated earth" allows you to camp anywhere you'd like for two days without the landowner's permission—as long as you're at least 150 meters (492 feet) from the house or cabin.

One holiday cabin in my family is a traditional, grass-roofed, cozy place with a view of three waterfalls and the majestic Hardanger glacier Jøkul.

Norway's most famous waterfall, the Vøringfoss, is a short distance from the hytte. *The fourth-generation Fossli Hotel overlooking the waterfall has been a favorite among vacationers, including composer Edvard Grieg. The hotel was built in 1890 with timber brought here by horseback from Eidfjord. For many years, only hikers could stay here. The road was not built until 1987.*

Onkel Johnny making får i kål.

✣
Mutton in Cabbage
får i kål

2 heads new cabbage (or about
   ½ cabbage per person)
4 pounds mutton (or about
   ¾ pound per person)
salt
whole peppercorns

1. Quarter the cabbage.
2. Place the cuts of meat with the most fat at the bottom of a large pot.
3. Cover the layer of meat with cabbage leaves. Sprinkle 1 tablespoon salt and several whole peppercorns over leaves.
4. Continue to layer the meat, cabbage, and salt and pepper. When the pot is full, pour enough water to fill the pot at least halfway. Be sure you can see the water in the pot to ensure that the dish does not taste dry.
5. Cover. Bring to a boil. Reduce heat and let simmer until the meat is thoroughly cooked, about 1½ hours. Shake the pot a few times during cooking to avoid sticking. Do not stir.

Serve hot with homemade flatbread, beer, and aquavit.

MAKES 5 TO 6 SERVINGS.

Such a popular dish inevitably has more than one recipe. The official recipe for *får i kål* given by the Royal Ministry of Foreign Affairs follows the same recipe that Johnny does. Before serving, however, it suggests adding some flour mixed with cold water to thicken the broth. It also suggests that you add margarine if your bottom layer of meat is not fatty enough. Finally, pour 2 cups of boiling water over the cabbage.

🦌

> *F*ood and clothes
> *Are needed for the man*
> *Who has travelled the mountains.*
> *Water and towels*
> *He can expect*
> *When he is invited to the table.*
>
> —Odin, Viking god, from the
> *Viking Cookbook*

*I*t was undoubtedly the Vikings who put Norway on the map. Although the Viking period seems to span thousands of years, they only ruled for about 200 years before the arrival of Christianity persuaded the chieftains to pack up and move house. The young Viking king Harald Fairhair, who vowed not to cut his hair until all of Norway was his, united the country in A.D. 872. His main incentive was to win the hand of the beautiful Gyda, who had announced she would only wed the ruler of all Norway. He did marry her—and several others.

As you can see by the words above of the greatest Viking god Odin, life was civilized in the days of the Vikings. Even the terrified monks in England, Ireland, and France, who described the Vikings as ruthless, observed that they were well-dressed and combed their hair and beards; combs made from reindeer antler are often found in Viking graves. As a host, you were extremely generous—and guests were modest and respectful. People kept animals and farmed the land. They hunted and fished, and their cuisine was so highly developed that many traditional Viking dishes are still enjoyed today.

The epic poem *Håvamål* expresses the principles of the Viking society, which focus on hospitality, the value of a good name, and friendship:

> *If a friend thou has whom thou fully wilt trust,*
> *Then fare to find him oft:*
> *For brambles grow and waving grass*
> *On the rarely trodden road.*

The Vikings made history by "colonizing" lands in a rapid and terrifying manner. It did not start off that way. Indeed, the Vikings only began to travel when they discovered their need for more farmland. It was under the Vikings that the interior farming districts became increasingly populated; this growth in population has sometimes been attributed to climactic warming, which in turn forced people to take to the seas. Increased numbers of family farms were more often divided for individuals. Even an unmarried woman or *mær* (the plural is *meyjar*) might build a home of her own, as is indicated by the name Møyarstader. The standard of living was also rising.

Although the Vikings had been trading for centuries, their oar-driven boats were soon discarded when they learned how to hoist a sail. The unique construction of their ships also enabled the Vikings to take their boats into shallow waters and even up on the beaches of the foreign countries. The word *Viking* may have come from the Norse word *vik* "inlet, bay," and *ing* "frequenter of": "one who came out from, or frequented, inlets of the sea" (*Oxford English Dictionary*).

Every May the Viking men left Norway to trade fur, ceramics, and young women in such faraway lands as the Byzantium, the Arab world, and North Africa, to Greenland, Iceland, and North America. They returned in the autumn. In the meantime, the women wove, harvested, and made the sails for the next year's trips. The symbol of the powerful housewife was her keys, hung from her belt, which were even buried with the woman. Indeed, the only key that the wife did not get was the key to the liquor cabinet.

Farmers, pioneers, and warriors, the Vikings were also very superstitious. Life after death was thought to be a continuation of life on earth; weapons, tools, jewelry, even animals, followed the dead into the grave. Those who died in battle went to Valhalla to fight all day and feast all night with Odin the Wise. The wights (*vetter*), invisible guardian spirits, populated their lands; the Vikings removed the figureheads from their ships upon their return home in order not to frighten the *vetter* away. Horses, which were particularly sacred, were carved on Viking furniture and boats in order to protect the household.

Many positive customs from the Vikings are still thriving in Norway— including their democratic way of administering law and order. Their meeting places, known as Things (still the name of Parliament Norway today, "Big Thing," or *Storting*), were civilized places used to settle disputes.

Less popular legal practices like *Jernbyrd*, the carrying of hot irons to prove innocence, have not lasted. King Harald Gille, who ruled from 1130 to 1136, actually is said to have earned his right to the throne by walking on hot irons.

Some Viking lore, on the other hand, isn't true. For example, although they were warriors, the Vikings did not wear helmets with the devilish horns on them that we see on Viking paraphernalia today. In the nineteenth century, to emphasize the horrors of Viking history, European opera houses added horns to traditional Viking helmets.

The Viking Museum in Oslo is a first-rate place to learn about the Vikings and their way of life. The contents of the Oseberg ship on display at the museum, such as furniture, wooden bowls, and baking materials, reveal a great deal about life with the Vikings. The ship is believed to be the grave of Ase, wife of the ninth-century king Gudrod Storlatnes and mother of Halfdan the Black (see page 169). All the Viking graves were hermetically sealed in blue clay, and their contents remained intact.

In 1981 a farmer from Borg ploughed into the remnants of a prehistoric settlement and discovered the largest Viking Age building ever found in Scandinavia (83 by 9 meters—272 × 29 feet). Studies show that the building was used for more than 500 years and dates as early as A.D. 400. Its size indicates that a chieftain or prince lived there with his family and servants. The building had been abandoned by the year 900, which also marks the end of the age of chieftains in Norway. Today it is a museum. Call ahead to arrange a Viking feast.

VIKINGLOVA

1. *Ver modig og paagaande.*
   Gaa rett paa sak.
   Grip sjansen som byr seg.
   Bruk fleire angrepsvinklar.
   Ver allsidig og modig.
   Angrip eitt maal om gongen.
   Ikkje planlegg alt i detaljar.
   Bruk dei beste vaapna.

2. *Ver kampklar.*
   Hald vaapna i orden.
   Hald deg i form.
   Finn gode kampfellar.
   Ver samde om hovudsaker.
   Velg ein hoovding.

3. *Ver ein god handelsmann.*
   Finn ut kva kjooparane har bruk for.
   Lov ikkje meir enn du kan halde.
   Ta ikkje for mykje betalt.
   Innrett deg saa du kan komme igjen.

4. *Hald leiren i orden.*
   Hald orden og oversikt.
   Gjer trivelege ting som styrker flokken.
   Sørg for at fleire gjer nyttige ting.
   Be all i flokken om raada deira.

The Laws of the Vikings

1. Be brave and aggressive.
    Be direct.
    Grab all opportunities.
    Use varying methods of attack.
    Be versatile and agile.
    Attack one target at a time.
    Don't plan everything in detail.
    Use top quality weapons.

2. Be prepared.
    Keep weapons in good condition.
    Keep in shape.
    Find good battle comrades.
    Agree on important points.
    Choose one chief.

3. Be a good merchant.
    Find out what the market needs.
    Don't promise what you can't keep.
    Don't demand overpayment.
    Arrange things so that you can return.

4. Keep the camp in order.
    Keep things tidy and organized.
    Arrange enjoyable activities that strengthen the group.
    Make sure everybody does useful work.
    Consult all members of the group for advice.

Reprinted from Mykle Illustrasjoner A/S—PR Produksjon A/S—Aasgaard Norge.

*T*he Vikings ate well and feasted on charcoal-grilled sheep's head, a dish of horsemeat, or veal roasted whole for festival occasions. The *Viking Cookbook* provides the following recipe.

Many legends of the beautiful ptarmigan (grouse) also originated during the Black Death (bubonic plague), which struck Norway in 1349. The Black Death was often personified as an old woman traveling the country with a rake and a broom. Where she raked, some survived, but where she swept, all were swept away. One community was entirely wiped out by the plague—except for one woman. For a long time she believed herself to be the last person left alive in the world. One day, however, she saw a man coming over the mountains. He believed her shouts of joy to be the sound of the *ryper* (ptarmigan or white grouse). Today the valley is called Rypdal, or Ptarmigan Valley.

✢
Roasted Grouse

2 grouse, plucked and cleaned
butter
1 or 2 teaspoons salt
1 teaspoon black pepper
1 cup stock

SAUCE

1½ cups stock or grouse juice
3 tablespoons concentrated red currant juice
2 tablespoons all-purpose flour
¾ cup whipping cream
1 teaspoon thyme
salt and pepper
1½ or 2 cups red currants

1. Truss each bird for an even shape. Brown in butter over medium-high heat.
2. Season with salt and pepper. Add stock to saucepan. Cover and let simmer until meat is tender, about 1 hour.
3. Set aside and keep warm.
4. Mix stock with the juice and scrapings from the frying pan. Bring to a boil.
5. Add the red currant juice.
6. Mix the flour with a small amount of cold water. Add to pan. Add cream. Bring to a boil again. Boil for about 4 minutes.
7. Season with thyme, salt, and pepper.

Place red currants on a dish. Place roasted grouse on the berries. Serve with sauce and vegetables.

MAKES 4 SERVINGS.

✋
Norwegian Stew

lapskaus

*T*his is the perfect dish to use whenever you have leftovers—especially in the winter. The more vegetables, meat, and potatoes the better.

1 bunch leeks, chopped
3 tablespoons butter
1 pound sausage, cut in pieces
7 medium potatoes, peeled
3 cups stock or water
8 medium carrots, chopped
any meat leftovers
any leftover gravy
salt, pepper, parsley, garlic

1. Sauté leek in butter in a large pan.
2. Add sausage and 3 sliced potatoes. Add stock or water. Bring to a boil. Reduce heat.
3. Add 4 potatoes, halved or cut in thirds, and meat leftovers. Let simmer for about 30 minutes.
4. Add carrots, leftover gravy, and spices. If you do not have any leftover gravy on hand, make a simple one by mixing a bouillon cube, a dash of flour, and half-and-half together. Cook an additional 10 or 15 minutes.

Serve with *flatbrød.*

MAKES ABOUT 6 SERVINGS.

If you take a drive through the countryside of Norway, you'll be treated to a view of picturesque landscapes, crystal-clear fjords, and spotless farmsteads. I am always struck by the particular beauty of the stabbur that stands on each farm. These traditional store-houses, which also served as the guesthouse, were often adorned with the best tapestries, the finest furniture, and the most finely carved balconies and galleries. Today they are used for storage and for fermenting beer and homemade wine.

*M*uch of typical Norwegian cuisine was simply the result of necessity. Before the invention of freezers, the Norwegians were forced to find creative ways to store food so that it would last from harvest to spring. To last through the long winters meats and fish were dried, pickled, cured, salted, smoked, even sugared, and, of course, frozen. As a result, certain foods became extremely popular. Delicious *fenalår*, for example, cured leg of mutton, is one of Norway's national dishes and is often served in thin slices for the *koldt bord* (see page 9). *Sursteik*, roast marinated and tenderized in vinegar or sour milk, was also popular. *Smalahove* is yet another odd favorite. This meal of sheep's head, salted, dried, and then boiled, is an ancient dish still enjoyed by many in the countryside.

The following *pinnekjøtt*, dried mutton ribs steamed over a rack of birch twigs, originated in Western Norway and Trøndelag. This region offers not only mountains, rivers, and the country's most famous elk (see page 111), but it was also site of the battle of Stiklestad, where St. Olav died on July 29, 1030 (see page 254 for details). A church built 100 years after his fall still stands in commemoration, and the thirteenth-century Trøndelag state arms depicts the ax that he carried that day. An annual play recounts the battle. The Order of St. Olav is still the highest decoration awarded in Norway. Trøndelag also boasts the rare *Tindved*, which is similar to the rowanberry. This ancient plant still grows along the edge of the Gaula River. The orange berries taste best after a night of frost.

Because *pinnekjøtt* tends to have a lot of fat and bone, I recommend that you allow at least a pound of meat per person. This dish is especially good in winter.

❧
Twig Meat

pinnekjøtt

3 pounds mutton ribs

1. Divide the mutton chops by cutting along the ribs. Soak in cold water overnight.
2. Place birch twigs (with the bark removed) or a metal grate in the bottom of a saucepan.
3. Add a little water—barely enough to cover the twigs. Place ribs on top of the twigs.
4. Bring the water to a boil. Steam meat until tender and the meat loosens from the bone, about 2 hours. If necessary, add water.

Serve on a heated plate with boiled potatoes, cranberry sauce, mashed rutabaga, French mustard, and sausages.

MAKES 6 SERVINGS.

*F*or thousands of years, pork has been the most common winter dish in Norway. My friend Nina Koren, who is from Østlandet in the southeast, gave me the following family recipe for *medisterkaker* and *ribbe* (see page 261), a traditional local meal enjoyed year-round but without fail during the Christmas season.

Østlandet is a land of lakes and rivers sparkling amid rolling farmland and picturesque villages. Just north of Nina's hometown of Moss, known primarily for its glass blowing and ship building, lies the popular coastal town of Son. Son was the home of the eccentric nineteenth-century artist Karl Dornberger. "The Last Musketeer," as he referred to himself, guarded his home with attack dogs and hidden gun traps. A notorious practical joker, Dornberger, who had a wooden leg, would often frighten strangers by brandishing a knife and then stabbing it into the lower part of his leg as if it were his own flesh. His house offered other surprises like a suit of armor whose arm would raise and shake a battle-axe at guests. Rumor had it that he practiced Black Magic in his kitchen. Today his home is a quiet private residence.

Pork Meatballs

medisterkaker

2 pounds lean pork, roughly ground
1 tablespoon salt
1 tablespoon potato flour or cornstarch
1 teaspoon allspice
1 teaspoon pepper
whole milk
ribbe (see page 261)

1. Mix pork, salt, flour, allspice, and pepper together. Mix well.
2. Add milk until dough is a firm enough to form balls.
3. Bake with *ribbe* for 15 to 20 minutes.

Serve with whipped egg cream (see page 225) for dessert.

MAKES 4 SERVINGS.

*T*he most northerly town in the world is Hammerfest, which takes its name from *feste,* which means "mooring place," and *hammer,* "a steep cliff." In this land of gray moss and few trees, summers are short. Indeed, there is so much snow in winter that residents find snow not only inside their locked cars but even in the pockets of inner layers of clothes. Workers use long poles to search for the cars covered by snow before clearing the streets after a storm. With the cold comes wind, and poles line the streets for pedestrians, who must travel from one to the next by rope in order not to blow away. My aunt and uncle, who lived in Hammerfest for years, tell stories of guests spending many a night because they were not able to drive home in the snow.

Hammerfest, which sees little sunlight in winter, was the first town in northern Europe to have electric light. As the story goes, a city official visited Paris for an exhibition in 1890 and saw the display of the electric light. Delighted, he knew it would be perfect for his hometown and—more daring any of the other more skeptical European participants—purchased a model from the show. Hammerfest built the first water-driven power station in Europe, and by 1892 its streets were filled with light.

Long before electric light arrived, the houses on Norway's outer northern islands were made of wood with an opening for light in the middle of the roof. The opening was covered with a thin animal skin in winter. To train children to tolerate cold weather, parents removed the cover and placed four-day-old babies underneath the opening for snow to fall on them.

Yes, the winters are long and intense. The sporty Nordmen, however, have invented quite a few creative pastimes for these long months. If you find yourself in Hammerfest in winter, arrange a snow scooter safari or even spend the night in a Lappish *lavvo* (tent). You can also take an ice-fishing trip to Eldorado, where the lakes are full of trout perfect for the dish below. Hammerfest is also base of the Royal and Ancient Polar Bear Society, of which my aunt is a member; the society studies and protects the bear. Ironically the skin of the largest polar bear ever shot is on display in the Town Hall.

Finally, consider a cruise around the North Cape, or Nordkapp, named by the English explorer Richard Chancellor in 1553 as he drifted along the coast here trying to find the Northeast Passage from the Atlantic to the

Pacific. Although North Cape is regarded as the northernmost point in Europe, neighboring Knivskjellodden lies even farther north. There isn't even a road to Knivskjellodden, however, while hoards of tourists visit Nordkapp. As you drive up to Nordkapp, watch for the reindeer grazing on the side of the roads.

In recent years Honningsvåg, Nordkapp's main settlement, has challenged Hammerfest's status as the northernmost city in the world. Luckily for Hammerfest, the village of Honningsvåg does not yet have "city" status.

☙
Lapland Beef

Lappebiff *or* Finnbiff

Elisabeth Seljevold provided the following recipe.

butter or fat for frying
2 pounds reindeer, deer, or other wild animal (shoulder or steak, fresh or
    frozen), cut into small pieces
several tablespoons bacon
several tablespoons all-purpose flour
salt and pepper

1. If the meat is fresh, do not remove any of its natural juices. You will use them later for the stock.
2. Place butter or fat in frying pan over low heat.
3. When butter has melted slightly, cover the bottom of the pan with a layer of beef and a little bacon.
4. Sprinkle flour, salt, and pepper over the meat.
5. Place another layer of meat, flour, salt, pepper. When you've used all the meat and bacon (about three layers), pour about a cup of water into the pan.
6. Cover with a lid. Bring to a boil. If the meat was frozen, be sure that it has defrosted completely. Mix all ingredients well.
7. Cook for 1 hour. Add salt and pepper to taste. If the meat tastes dry, add water. If it is too watery in phe pan, add flour, salt, and pepper.

Good with a little sour cream and wild mushrooms. Serve with boiled potatoes, lingonberries, and green vegetables.

MAKES 4 SERVINGS.

MUSHROOMS

$\mathcal{E}$veryone loves to go mushroom picking in the fall. The popular chanterelle mushroom is particularly tasty with the previous recipe.

It was the author Asbjørnsen, famous for his collection of Norwegian folk tales, who introduced the Norwegians to the idea of eating mushrooms. He published the first recipes for mushrooms in *Sensible Cooking*. Although this controversial book was frowned upon for attacking many of Norway's ancient culinary traditions, it did promote an increased understanding of the health benefits provided by some vegetables.

Most popular mushrooms are the *blek piggsopp*, the hedgehog fungus, and the *ekte kantarell*, or chanterelle. The *sauesopp* is best when fried with onions and other spices. Also good are the *matriske*, or saffron milk cap, which exudes drops of orange milk when you scratch it, and the tasty *rødskrubb*, or orange birch bolete, which colors all food black.

A Note about Norway in a Nutshell

*Y*ou could spend years exploring the villages and fjords of Norway—or you could sign on for a four-day trip called Norway in a Nutshell. This ride into western Norway not only takes you through the natural beauty of the country but also provides easy access to the myriad of outdoor activities on offer. If you don't have time for the whole trip, take a daylong excursion outside Oslo. Really, it's one of the most beautiful train rides in the world. In addition, the trip is flexible. You can leave the train at any time and get back on hours—or even days—later.

Our first stop out of Oslo is Geilo, a spectacular little town and a good place to disembark—especially if you bring your skis with you. Geilo is a popular ski resort in winter, and you can follow one of the many ski runs from the train station any time of year. Ask for a guide at the Hangen Hotel, right beside the station. The Hallingskarvet Mountains, skiable only for experienced skiers, lie directly to your north. (Take your fishing pole, too; you'll find good trout fishing in the lakes in the area.)

The next stop is Haugastøl. You can cycle from here down the workmen's road toward Finse, the next train stop. Although parts of this road may be buried under snow even well into summer, you can follow the sticks that poke up through the snow marking the way until the road clears up again; August and September are good times to ride.

Finse has the most-elevated railway station in Norway. From it you can see the Hardanger-Jookulen glacier, which is covered with snow throughout the year. If you have the time, I recommend you spend the night at the hotel here (called Finse 1222 because that's the elevation of the glacier) or at the overnight tourist cottage a short walk away. Unlike the hotel, the cottage is open all year, and you don't need reservations. You'll always find a bed or a spot on the floor. You can't miss either place; the town of Finse consists only of a few buildings.

Ask for a map and a guide at the station at 1222 and walk or ski up to the glacier. You can stop in at Kjeldabu, one of the huts around the glacier, and serve yourself some lunch or pick up supplies on the way. If you have forgotten your bike, you can rent one at 1222 or at Haugastøl, your next station stop. The old construction road was originally laid to provide access for men and materials during the building of the mountain section of the railway.

The road follows the train tracks on to Myrdal, one of the most famous sights in Norway and the base for a spectacular ride. One of the steepest train rides in the world—a rickety 20-kilometer-long (12 miles), 900-meter-fall (2953 feet), 50-minute-long, and 55-degree elevation—the ride takes you down an exquisite mountainside into the Flåm Valley to the town of Flåm and the Aurlandsfjord. The old wooden train, famous throughout Norway for its unique craftsmanship and design (it has five brake systems for the steep hill), provides a bumpy ride, and you may prefer to ride your bike or walk down the steep hill. Either way, the scenery is exquisite—high waterfalls, spectacular cliffs, fields of wildflowers, and herds of sheep and goats will surround you.

When we arrive in tiny Flåm, a ferry is waiting, and we jump on for a trip around the Aurlandsfjord. Enormous cliffs rise up on either side, and tiny houses nestle between the waterfalls and crags. Sheep and goats graze precariously on the mountainside. Seals swim in the waters around us. Undredal, a tiny 123-person community on the shores of the fjord, accessible by car for the first time only 10 years ago, is home to the smallest church in Norway.

Far within the depths of the fjords is one Norwegian farmhouse sitting high up on the top of a cliff. We are told that the people who live there can only reach their home by a steep ladder from a dock below. One winter day a few years ago so much snow fell that the man of the house could not climb the ladder, and his wife had to stay alone on top of the cliff for four months.

The Undredal church is the smallest Scandinavian church still in use. First a stave church, it is believed to have been built in 1147.

Mama's Meatcakes

kjøttkaker

1 pound ground beef
1½ teaspoons salt
¼ teaspoon pepper
¼ teaspoon nutmeg
1 teaspoon ginger
2½ tablespoons potato flour or cornstarch
about 1 cup whole milk or water
butter for frying

1. Mix beef and salt together. Add pepper, nutmeg, ginger, and potato flour. Mix well.
2. Gradually add the milk or water.
3. Shape the mixture into round cakes. Heat pan and fry in butter over medium-high heat. Remove from pan.
4. Put enough water in a pot to cover the cakes. Bring to a boil. Transfer meat cakes to the pot. Simmer for about 10 minutes.

Serve with boiled potatoes, stewed green peas or cabbage, lingonberries, and thick brown gravy.

MAKES 4 SERVINGS.

✠

Boiled Lamb and Sausage

2 pounds salted and smoked lamb, sliced (preferably shoulder or leg)
1½ pounds smoked beef sausage (precooked)
1 rutabaga
5 ounces bacon
½ cup (1 stick) butter

1. Boil the lamb until tender, about 1½ hours.
2. Place the sausages in boiling water. Let simmer until warmed through.
3. Peel the rutabaga. Cut it into slices about ½ inch thick. Boil in salted water for about 30 minutes.
4. To make the bacon butter, cut the bacon into small (¼ inch) cubes and sauté in a frying pan until golden. Add the butter. When the butter has melted, the bacon butter is ready to serve.

Serve with potato dumplings (see page 198).

MAKES 4 SERVINGS.

✠

Lamb with Dill

*S*trong-tasting herbs are the perfect accompaniment to lamb.

4-pound lightly salted, smoked leg of lamb
stock vegetables (including carrots, leeks)
spices (celery, parsley, thyme, a bay leaf, and white pepper)
butter
all-purpose flour
bunch of fresh dill

1. Place lamb in a pan. Remove the knuckle end if necessary. Cover with cold water and bring to a boil.
2. Skim fat off the surface.
3. Reduce heat and let the lamb simmer for 30 minutes. Using low heat takes longer but gives a better result.
4. After 30 minutes, add more water if the stock tastes too salty. Add stock vegetables and spices. Continue to simmer for about 2 hours.
5. Strain the stock. Measure about 2 tablespoons butter and 1 or 2 tablespoons flour per each cup stock. Melt desired amount of butter. Add flour. Stir over low heat until brown. Add suitable amount of strained broth. Let simmer for 5 minutes. Add the chopped dill right before serving.

Good hot or cold, as a sandwich topping or in a salad.

MAKES 8 SERVINGS.

❧

Roast Leg of Lamb

2 teaspoon salt
1 teaspoon pepper
2 or 3 teaspoons crushed rosemary
1 clove garlic, finely chopped
5-pound leg of lamb
1 large onion
2 or 3 carrots
1 or 2 cups boiling water
4 tablespoons butter
5 tablespoons all-purpose flour
red wine (optional)

Preheat the oven to 250° F.

1. Rub salt, pepper, rosemary, and garlic well into lamb. Insert a roasting thermometer into the thickest part of the leg. Be sure that it doesn't touch the bone.
2. Place in baking dish. Peel the onion and cut it into segments.
3. Peel the carrots. Chop into small pieces. Place both onion and carrots into pan with the lamb.
4. Bake for 1 hour. Add boiling water. Continue to cook, allowing about 1 hour per pound.
5. Let lamb sit for 20 minutes before carving.
6. To make gravy, melt the butter and add the flour. Stir over low heat until brown. Add 5 cups juices from the cooked lamb or a mixture of juices and stock. Stir continuously while it comes to a boil. Add red wine if desired. Let gravy simmer, uncovered, for about 10 minutes. Add salt and pepper to taste.

Serve lamb with gravy and vegetables.

MAKES 6 TO 8 SERVINGS.

Do not complain under the stars of the dearth of bright points in your life.

—Henrik Wergeland

*T*he northern city of Tromsø is perhaps best known for its whaling station, which fills the town with the strong aroma of whaling oil. Thirteenth-century Tromsø is also the gateway to Finnmark, 48,000 square kilometers (18,500 square miles) of vast wilderness and home to the Sami and the reindeer (see page 153). Its forbidding terrain is a tough place to eke out a living. Dairy farming provides the most opportunities for these hardy Norwegians. The only problem they face is the unusual abundance of Siberian garlic found in the area. If farmers aren't careful, the cows will devour it and give their milk the taste of onions.

Largely because of a year-round ice-free harbor, Tromsø became a major fishing port and trading station in the eighteenth century. Today the town's Polaria museum is famous. Its showcase of Polar attractions offers a polar walk from Svalbard and a display of the northern lights that is just as spectacular as the real thing. In January the city hosts a Northern Lights Festival, which features classical and contemporary music. A statue of Roald Amundsen, the Norwegian explorer who was the first man to reach the South Pole, also testifies to the many Arctic expeditions that left from Tromsø. It was also here that King Håkon proclaimed a "Free Norway" before being forced into exile during World War II.

Be sure to stop in at the Tromsø Jernbanestasjon, or Tromsø Railway Station, a pub designed just like one—although the town does not (yet) actually have a station!

A specialty of the region is *mackøl* and hardboiled *måsegg*. This is the only place where the *mås* bird is found. Locals enjoy it with *mackøl*, which has been brewed in the region for 120 years. The beer was the first Norwegian beer to be distributed to all the counties of Norway and to be sold in Sweden and Finland.

Norway gained sovereignty of the polar island group of Svalbard in 1925. Its name means "land of the cold coast." Polar bears are so abundant in the northern region of Svalbard that road signs warn of their passing. Almost two-thirds of the land is covered by glaciers. Mining is the main industry; seal hunting and fishing are close seconds.

The weather is tough for the small population of Svalbard. Although the mid-night sun is visible from April 21 to August 21, the sun doesn't shine at all from October 28 to February 14. The islands offer outdoor adventures of a lifetime if you're interested— or take a flight around the area for an aerial view.

Fridtjof Nansen, Roald Amundsen, and Otto Sverdrup laid the foundations here for Norway's position as a polar nation. In 1888 Nansen, Sverdrup, and four others skied across the ice cap covering hitherto unknown inland Greenland. The next voyage went even farther north. Nansen planned to let his vessel, the Fram, *freeze in the ice, believing that it would drift with the ice from Siberia across the Arctic Circle to Greenland. The* Fram *sailed north in the summer of 1893 and entered the ice off the New Siberian Islands. After drifting for over a year, Nansen left the vessel to attempt to reach the North Pole on skis and with dogs. After four months on the ice, they arrived at Franz Josef Land, where they spent the winter planning to cross the Barents Sea to Svalbard in kayaks the following summer. Their expedition was delayed, however, and they arrived at the same time as the* Fram, *which had emerged from the ice off Svalbard after a three-year voyage. You can visit the* Fram *and climb through the decks on Bygdøy peninsula in Oslo.*

SIDE DISHES FOR MEAT

❧

Creamed Peas

stuete erter

1¼ cups dried peas
½ cup whole milk
1 tablespoon all-purpose flour
salt

1. Soak peas overnight.
2. Boil peas in fresh water until soft, about 10 minutes.
3. Mix peas, milk, and flour. Reduce heat and let simmer for 5 or 6 minutes.
4. Add salt to taste.

MAKES 3 OR 4 SERVINGS.

❧
Stewed Potatoes with Dill I

stuete poteter

2 pounds potatoes (about 6 medium), peeled and sliced
1 cup cream
1 cup whole milk
1 teaspoon mustard
salt and pepper
½ cup chopped dill

1. Boil potatoes in cream and milk until cooked, 6 to 10 minutes. Add mustard, salt, and pepper to taste.
2. When the sauce begins to thicken, add chopped dill. After several minutes, remove from heat.

Serve immediately. Also accompanies fish dishes.

MAKES 4 SERVINGS.

Stewed Potatoes with Dill II

12 medium potatoes, peeled and diced
3 tablespoons butter
3 tablespoons all-purpose flour
2 cups whole milk
salt
white pepper
dill

1. Bring the potatoes to a boil. Reduce heat and let simmer until cooked, 6 to 10 minutes. Drain and set aside.
2. Melt butter in a frying pan over medium heat.
3. When foam subsides, stir in flour and simmer for 2 minutes. Remove from heat.
4. Add milk to pan. Stir vigorously to blend ingredients thoroughly. Place pan over moderate heat. Stir until sauce comes to a boil. Reduce heat and simmer 5 to 10 minutes, stirring occasionally. Pour over potatoes.
5. Add salt, pepper, and dill to taste.

MAKES 12 TO 15 SERVINGS.

✂
Stewed Cabbage

stuet kål

1 pound garden cabbage, diced
½ teaspoon salt
2 tablespoons butter
4 tablespoons all-purpose flour
2 cups whole milk
½ teaspoon nutmeg

1. Cook cabbage until tender in salted water, about 30 minutes. Drain and set the cabbage water aside.
2. Melt the butter in a saucepan over low to medium heat. Stir in the flour. Add milk and bring to a boil, stirring constantly. Simmer for 8 to 10 minutes.
3. Add cabbage to the sauce and mix. Bring to a boil. Season with salt and nutmeg.

MAKES 4 SERVINGS.

❧

Red Cabbage and Apples

surkål

*P*opular for Christmas dinner. Especially good with pork and *ribbe.*

½ cup (1 stick) butter
2 or 3 small (2 large) red cabbages, shredded
several tablespoons caraway seeds
4 apples, peeled and chopped into small pieces
sugar and vinegar
salt and pepper

1. Melt butter over low heat.
2. Layer red cabbage, caraway seeds, and apples.
3. Sprinkle sugar and vinegar over the dish.
4. Cook at least 2 hours over low heat. Taste every once in a while. You may need additional caraway seeds, sugar, or vinegar. Add more sugar, vinegar and/or salt and pepper to taste.

MAKES 8 TO 10 SERVINGS.

Soups

I Jesu navn: Går vi til bords.
Spise og drikke på ditt ord.
Deg Gud til ære:
Oss til gavn.
Så får vi mat i Jesu navn.
Amen.

In Jesus' name we go to the table
And eat and drink by your word.
To honor our God to us is a pleasure.
We receive this meal in Jesus' name.
Amen.

—Old Norwegian blessing

❧

*If you get lost in life, put your ear to the ground and listen to
its pounding heart.*
— Old Sami saying

Perhaps Norway's most fascinating region is Lapland, or Finnmark,
home to the Lapps, or Sami, a nomadic people who still practice a way of
life that is thousands of years old. The word *Sami* comes from *sampi*, which
means both the land and the people. These aboriginal people of Norway
consider themselves Sami first and Norwegians second. They speak their
own language, which has three different dialects, and are fiercely protective
of their culture. The Norwegian government supports their culture. A 1751
peace treaty, the Lappekodicillen, protected the Sami's grazing rights to the
frontier areas and was meant to protect reindeer herding. More effective
was the recent establishment of the Sami Parliament, the *Sameting*, in 1989
in Karasjok, Norway's Sami capital.

About 20,000 Sami live in Finnmark today. With the brightly colored gar-
ments and unique, knee-bended walk that comes from a lifetime spent on
skis, they are easy to spot. The main groups are the River Sami, who depend
on fishing for their main source of income; the Sea Sami, who live by agriculture and fishing; and the Mountain Sami, who breed reindeer. Sami are
most notable for the domestication of reindeer; most of the 40% of Norway's
land mass used for reindeer grazing is in Finnmark. The seriousness of reindeer herding is evident from notices displayed around the region:

You are now in reindeer herding district.
*Reindeer herding is an industry from prehistoric times in this part of the
country and reserved for the Lapps, a privilege established by law.*
*The taming of reindeer is beset with difficulties, and the Lapps would
appreciate it if you would cooperate.*
*Do not approach grazing reindeer. You may frighten the females away from
the calves and scatter the flock.*
*Ask permission if you wish to approach a reindeer fence when work among
reindeer is going on.*

Keep away and do not approach a flock being driven by. Driver, do not increase speed after a reindeer on the road—it will become reluctant to leave the road, and on the point of exhaustion may turn on the car.
At night lower the lights and drive with care.

—Excerpted from *Norway* by Barbara Øvstedal

These notices are no joke. Many polar animals like reindeer survive the winter because of the fat they put on during summer. If their summer feeding is disturbed they can face serious trouble in winter; lack of energy can be especially critical in late winter. Animals frightened while hunting or grazing at that time of year may not survive until summer.

Every spring more than 200 Sami depart from Kautokeino, the center of the largest reindeer district and host to two annual reindeer markets, to follow herds of about 50,000 head of reindeer to the coast. They live in *lavvoes* (tents) and travel at night, when the snow is frozen hard. Slaughtering takes place in September, and they are back home in time for Christmas.

The Sami enjoy life and are not afraid of taking their time doing so. A traveler once told the story of his car breaking down near a *lavvoe*. The Lapps saw him and he eagerly took them up on their offer to take him to his destination. First, however, they insisted that he enjoy a meal with them. After the meal he urged them to begin their journey, as he was in a hurry. They pleasantly agreed but first served a round of coffee. He quickly drank it and pressed again to leave. They settled down to enjoy an after-dinner smoke, remarking that if he was in such a hurry, he should've broken his car down the day before! If you, too, decide to travel along the Finnmarksvidda, the best time to go is in August and early September when the mosquitoes are gone and the weather is still mild.

Sami are also known for their herbal medicines. They use both animal and vegetable products in their medicines, and many healers still practice their ancient art, often combining their knowledge with local health personnel. In cases where a diagnosis is uncertain, the *noiade* might seek advice from his shamanic drum, or *runebommen,* and transcend consciousness to cure sickness.

Be sure to look for the beautiful Sami jewelry. One of the best stores is Juhlsmie, located in Kautokeino and in Oslo beside the city hall. The Sami also sell in booths along the main street of Kautokeino.

The reindeer shapes the Sami cuisine. Every part is enjoyed. Boiled marrowbone, brain sausage, and blood pudding are only a few traditional Sami dishes.

❧

Reindeer Stew

bidos

1 pound reindeer meat, chipped (substitute: any other meat appropriate
   for stews)
2 or 3 tablespoons butter for frying
1 onion, chopped
2 teaspoons cornstarch
4 small potatoes, diced (optional)
4 carrots, diced (optional)
3 slices *geitost*
1 teaspoon salt
½ teaspoon pepper
a few crushed cranberries (optional)
10 crushed juniper berries (optional)
fried mushrooms (optional)
flour
2 teaspoons sour cream

1. Separate the reindeer meat into three portions. If you are using frozen reindeer, do not thaw before cooking. Warm a frying pan and melt butter in the pan. Brown the first third of the meat in butter. Remove and set aside in a large pot.
2. Brown the remaining two sections of meat, scraping the pan in between portions with a few tablespoons water and adding 1 tablespoon of butter. Place the cooked meat in the pan.
3. Add 2 cups water and scrape the pan. Add the onion and sauté until translucent. Finally, add the cornstarch to thicken the soup. Add potatoes and carrots if desired.

4. Simmer until meat is tender, about 15 minutes.
5. Add *geitost*, salt, pepper, berries, and mushrooms to taste. The berries give it the wild taste many Norwegians love. For a thicker sauce, mix a small amount of flour and water together and add to sauce.
6. Add sour cream just before serving.

Serve with boiled potatoes, brussels sprouts, lingonberry sauce, and flatbread.

MAKES 2 OR 3 SERVINGS.

*T*he following recipe came from our friend Joan Werness Martin, whose grandfather took the name Werness in the 1890s when he came to America from Værnes Kirke in Hell, near Trondheim. So many Norwegians emigrated to the United States and Canada from 1825 to 1930 (almost 900,000) that today there are as many Norwegian-Americans on this side of the Atlantic as there are people in Norway. If you have roots you would like to trace in Norway, contact the Norwegian Emigration Center for assistance.

The town of Hell—the word actually means good fortune in Norwegian—is a popular tourist destination—not only because of its name (who wouldn't want to send a postcard from Hell?) but also for its beauty. Joan has been following her grandmother's and great-grandmother's recipes of local cuisine for many years.

🍲
Fruit Soup

fruktsuppa

½ box (7.5 ounces) dried apricots
½ box (7.5 ounces) prunes
¼ box (4 ounces) raisins
½ package (4 ounces) dried apple slices
½ can (10 ounces) sliced peaches, drained (optional)
¼ to ½ cup sugar
½ cinnamon stick
1 slice orange with rind
½ slice lemon (¼ inch) with rind
1 or 2 whole cloves
1 tablespoon quick-cooking tapioca
whipped cream (optional)

1. Place the first 10 ingredients (apricots to cloves) in a large stainless steel or enamel pot.
2. Add water to cover fruit and let simmer until fruit is plump and tender.
3. Remove from heat and add tapioca. Mix thoroughly. Let cool and refrigerate. The soup should be the consistency of a thick pudding.
4. Serve soup cold, with whipped cream if desired, as a dessert or a side dish. Fruit soup can also be served as a breakfast soup. When serving for breakfast, serve without whipped cream.

MAKES ABOUT 10 (⅔-CUP) SERVINGS.

*F*ish soup is a staple of every Norwegian diet. Indeed, every house and hotel seem to have its own recipe. I've probably eaten twenty different kinds of fish soup in all my trips to Norway. If you decide to serve it for company, I suggest that you use the creamy white-sauce recipe given below. For everyday meals, serve with fish balls or pieces of fish.

One of the best areas to taste fish soup is in the Lofoten Islands, a gorgeous mountainous archipelago located just above the Arctic Circle. Although residents concoct creative recipes from the berries and juicy green fodder from the mountains, it is the fishing industry to which their lives are linked. Thanks to the Gulf Stream, the islands enjoy mild winters and temperate waters, which attract Norwegian Arctic cod and other fish to the region.

On my last visit to Lofoten, I tasted a variation of fish soup at every meal. Yes, it is always delicious and, no, never quite the same. The proprietors at the Rica Hotel in Svolvær, for example, who recently won a prize for their soup, swear that the secret is to make fish stock from the entire fish—head and all. They use the cod that arrives here every spring. You can actually fish for cod from one of the hotel's 1800-kroner (about $250 a day) rooms. The rooms, built just a few feet over the water, are designed with a fishing hole in the center of the floor. The hotel will provide fishing equipment, and the chef will cook up your catch for you in a delicious—yes— fish soup. (You can fish for your dinner at many other locales as well, including the fisheries museum on the island of Hjertøya.)

To make a simple fish soup, follow this basic recipe: Boil fish with vegetables for ½ hour. Strain the fish for the broth, and add real cream before you serve it. More complicated fish soups call to place codfish bones and salmon bones with vegetables (carrots, onions, leeks, celery) and herb (bay leaves, white pepper, and thyme) in ice-cold water before bringing it to a boil. After straining the broth, add more carrots, onions, and leeks, and let simmer. For this recipe, add crème fraîche and fresh cod pieces before serving.

❧
Fish Soup

4 or 5 tablespoons butter
6 tablespoons all-purpose flour
4 cups fish stock, heated
salt
pepper
1 small carrot
1 or 2 tablespoons chopped leeks
12 peeled shrimp
12 mussels or scallops
3 ounces catfish or monkfish, steamed
½ cup heavy cream
2 tablespoons sour cream
2 teaspoons lumpfish caviar

1. Melt 2½ tablespoons butter. Mix in the flour. Stir in the hot fish stock.
2. Bring to a boil. Reduce heat slightly and let gently boil for about 10 minutes.
3. Season with salt and pepper.
4. Cut carrots and leeks into thin strips. Sauté in the rest of the butter, and add to the soup.
5. Add shrimp, mussels or scallops, catfish or monkfish, and cream.
6. Serve with sour cream and caviar.

MAKES 4 SERVINGS.

I must confess that I ate whale during a stay in the lovely little fishing town of Henningsvær, the "Venice of the North." My hosts at the fabulous Henningsvær Bryggehotel prepared it for me. Sliced very fine and salted and sugared, it was absolutely delicious.

Politically incorrect or not, whaling has been an industry here for generations. The headquarters of the whaling organization "High North Alliance" is located in neighboring Reine, which has more whaling licenses than anywhere else in the country. Andenes, located at the northern tip of Vesteralen Islands, Lofoten's northern neighbors, is famous for its whale safaris, during which a marine biologist will take you for a six-hour trip offshore for a nearly guaranteed sighting of sperm, killer, and minke whales. Because explorers have overhunted whales since the seventeenth century, some species face extinction today. In those days one whale was valuable enough to pay for the entire expedition. Whale oil was used in lamps, as a lubricant, and for soap.

The Bryggehotel invites guests to take their boat the Symra for a fishing trip. Their talented chef will prepare your catch for a meal. Although there is no guarantee you will catch anything, one local fisherman said, "You'd have to be lucky to come home empty-handed."

Just across the harbor is the Finnholmen Brygge, part of a year-round fish landing station that also offers comfortable rooms. In addition, Lofoten's mountaineering school Den Siste Viking offers rooms. Climbers here face the 40-meter-high (131-foot) "Svolvær goat," a 1-meter-wide (3-foot) ravine shaped like the horns of a goat that is situated at a steep mountain peak. It gives me the willies just to think of it.

𝒩orway's ancient capital of Trondheim is the country's third-largest city. The city, which celebrated its 1000th birthday in 1997, was known until the sixteenth century as Nidaros, or "the mouth of the river Nid."

Trondheim was built on the burial site of Viking Olav Haraldsson. As the story goes, Olav Haraldsson, a notorious Viking like the ones before him, served as mercenary in Normandy and England. There he converted to Christianity. When he invaded Norway in 1015 and became king, he ordered the desecration of all pagan sites and the execution of those who refused baptism. Not surprisingly, he was intensely disliked and eventually forced into exile.

Two years later Olav returned to fight at the battle of Stiklestad (see page 254) near Trondheim, where he died. The Stiklestad Nasjonale Kultursenter marks the spot. The fight for Christianity wasn't over yet, however. Reports of strange goings on at his burial site led to the exhumation of his body a year later. Incredibly his body had not decayed—and his hair and finger-nails had actually grown. He was placed in a silver casket in the town's little wooden church and declared a saint. In 1066 King Olav Kyrre ordered a cathedral to be built on the site. The Nidaros Domkirke, Scandinavia's largest medieval building, is still a site for pilgrimages. All kings of Norway are crowned in this cathedral.

About 2 kilometers (1¼ miles) off the shore of Trondheim is Munkholmen (Monk's Island), an island used as a Viking execution ground and as a showcase for the heads of St. Olav's enemies. An eleventh-century Bene-dictine monastery, one of the first two in Scandinavia, was built here; it failed after the archbishop received complaints about womanizing and drinking. After the Reformation it was converted into a prison and then a customs office. Today stone walls encircle the island.

Following is Lisa Anne Yayla's family recipe for Trondheim soup.

Trondheim Nose Burner Soup

1 pound meat, cubed
vegetable oil or butter for frying
any peeled vegetables (for example: potatoes, carrots)
salt, pepper

1. Brown meat in oil or butter.
2. Add water to cover about 1 inch above the meat. Bring to a boil.
3. Add vegetables. Simmer until vegetables are tender and meat is cooked.
4. Season with salt and pepper.

Serve with *knekkebrød*. This dish is even better the day after you make it.

MAKES ABOUT 4 SERVINGS.

On the way to the Holmenkollen Ski Festival, which takes place on the second Sunday in March every year. About 60,000 people attend; most walk to the Holmenkollen ski jump as no cars are allowed and the trams are full. Hot chocolate, matpakke, *and warmclothes are a must. Contact Stryn Sommarskisenter to arrange a summer ski trip.*

*I*n Norwegian mythology Ull is the god of skiing and Skade the goddess of skiing and hunting. A 4000-year-old rock carving of skiers found in northern Norway is a testament to the ancient history of skiing in this Nordic land. Indeed, skis, the only practical means of transportation during winter, were indispensable when hunting, trapping, or fishing.

The Holmenkollen ski jump, site of the 1952 Olympics and host of frequent concerts and ski meetings today, houses Oslo's Ski Museum. The museum, which boasts the oldest collection of skiing gear in the world, is home to the 2500-year-old Ovrebo ski and the rock carving of skiers found at Rødøy. The first pair of skis consisted of a 9-foot-long ski and a second shorter one covered in animal skins for effective kicking. Skis of the same length did not become popular until the 1700s; 100 years later, Sondre Norheim of Telemark, who became known as the "Father of Skiing," revived interest in skiing as a sport and made the first jump in skis. Norheim ended 4000 years of tradition by using stiff ski bindings. He also combined cross-country skiing with jumping and slalom. Even the word *slalom* originated in his home of Morgedal, a popular ski resort town. The first syllable means "slope," and *lam* means "track down the slope." Norheim's home is now a museum. Norheim also designed the "waisted ski," which is the prototype of the skis used today, and eventually immigrated to America. He and Norwegian Jon Torsteinson (Snowshoe Thompson) of Telemark promoted skiing in the States.

Geilo, Hemsedal, Oppdal, and Voss are the main downhill resorts in Norway today. Cross-country skiing, on the other hand, is simply a part of life. Many Norwegians still use skis to get to school and work.

*L*ike King Olav V, father of the present king and a true Nordman in his love for snow, many Norwegians have jumped from the 183-foot Holmenkollen ski jump since the 1952 Olympics. King Olav V once opened the Holmenkollen ski meeting with the first jump. I can only recommend the amazingly realistic simulator located underneath the jump.

The well-loved King Olav, himself the winner of an Olympic gold medal in sailboat racing in 1928, was known as the people's king. He often took long walks or ski trips around Oslo's countryside with no guards to protect him. One Norwegian tells a story of passing him on a cross-country trail outside the city. Soon after, he passed a small boy on skis. "Ski quickly," he told the boy, "and you'll catch up with the king." "I know," replied the boy. "He's my father." An American journalist once questioned him about the risk in taking such unguarded walks. "I have 4½ million Norwegians to protect me," was the king's famous reply.

The small boy on skis is now King Harald V, the first prince in 567 years to be born in Norway. He made even more of a splash when he married a commoner. Crown Prince Harald met Sonja Haraldsen when he was a student at the Norwegian Military Academy. She was the daughter of an Oslo shop owner. They agreed to wait ten years before marrying, after which time King Olav finally approved the match. Norway is a constitutional monarchy. Although the king has no real power, the royal family has the total support of the Norwegian people. Legislative power is exercised by the national assembly, the Storting, which is elected every four years.

My parents honeymooned at the romantic Holmenkollen Park Hotel forty Christmases ago.

Here is my family at Holmenkolldagen.

$\mathcal{M}$y mother was born in Oslo, the capital of Norway. The word Oslo comes from the Norse word for God, *As*, and *Lo*, which means field. This beautiful city was reputedly founded in 1048 as a strategic military site for Harald Hardråde the Hard, who fought alongside Olav at Stiklestad and was known for making his enemies "kiss the thin lips of the axe." Recent archeological finds, however, indicate that Oslo might be fifty years older. The agreeable Norwegians declared this a very good reason to celebrate Oslo's 1000th anniversary in the year 2000. I feel certain that they look forward to celebrating again in another fifty years!

Still, Oslo considers Harald Hardråde its founder, and a sculptured relief of him riding a horse hangs on the west wall of the town hall. Medieval Oslo was situated beneath the Ekeberg heights at the mouth of the River Alna, about 3 kilometers (1¾ miles) east of today's city center. By A.D.1300 the old town had a population of about 3000. Although the kings of Norway did not yet reside in Oslo, Hardråde's son Olav Kyrre built a cathedral here; the city boasted two palaces, one for the bishop and one for the king. In the fourteenth century King Håkon V finally did move to Oslo and built the Akershus fortress, one of the few structures in Norway built of stone rather than wood. Today you can visit the Resistance Museum located at the castle, which tells the story of Norway's struggle against German occupation during World War II.

Oslo prospered until the plague struck its citizens in 1349. It didn't truly thrive again until after the Great Fire of 1624 when its Danish King Christian V took such an interest in it that he changed its name to his own, Christiania, and moved it 3 kilometers to its present location. It would not be named Oslo again until 1924.

The city's best museums are located on the Bygdøy peninsula, to which ferries shuttle from the Rådhus, or City Hall. They include the Viking Museum, with a display of ninth-century ships excavated throughout Norway, including the Oseberg and Gokstad ships and their contents; the Kon-Tiki Museum, detailing the journey Thor Heyerdahl made across the Pacific; and the Fram museum (see page 144). Also be sure to visit the Nasjonalgalerie, Munch museum, which boasts a superb collection of the artist's work, and Frognerparken, home to most of Gustav Vigeland's sculptures.

Dinner at Bygdøy peninsula.

Oslo's coat of arms depicts St. Hallvard, the city's patron saint, holding three arrows and a millstone and seated on a lion-headed stool. A woman lies at his feet. As the story goes, the young noblemen was about to cross the fjord one day when a pregnant woman approached him and begged to be saved from being killed for a theft she did not commit. He believed her and rowed her in the direction of his father's house. Unfortunately the attackers killed them with arrows. Although they tied his body to a millstone, however, he did not sink. He was proclaimed a saint.

For a better understanding of life in Norway centuries ago, visit the Norwegian Folk Museum, the largest national museum of cultural history in the country. Nearly 200 years old, it comprises an open-air display of 140 dwellings and farm buildings and offers indoor collections of folk art and lore, including a collection of love gifts given to boys from girls when it was still considered improper to be seen together during the day.

Oslo street scene.

The Oslofjord links the capital to the open sea and has long been one of Norway's busiest waterways. The countryside around Oslo is rich with gentle hills, picturesque towns, and farming communities. About an hour outside Oslo is the Hadeland glass factory, a good place to buy presents for every occasion. On the drive to the factory you'll pass the gravesite of Halfdan the Black. This Viking king drowned in the Randsfjord on his way to a Christmas Eve party. King Halfdan was so popular that when he died the people divided his body into four parts so that every region could have a piece of the king to ensure the fertility of the land. Legend has it that his head is buried in the gravesite outside Oslo.

Some 80 kilometers (50 miles) from Oslo is Eidsvoll, where on August 14, 1814, at the Moss Convention Norwegian leaders met with Danish Crown Prince Christian Frederick to decide whether to accept union with Sweden or to seat Christian Frederick on the throne. They chose independence. Norway remained an independent nation under the Swedish crown until 1905, when it became truly independent.

⚶

Oslo Soup

Norway's Delight provided the following recipe.

2 cups prunes
1 cup oats
2 cups fruit juice
¼ cup sugar

1. Soak prunes in water overnight.
2. Boil the oats and prunes in 8 cups water for about an hour. Add the juice and sugar.

MAKES 7 OR 8 SERVINGS.

Glassblower at Hadeland glass works.

Breads, Pancakes, and Dumplings

I was lying awake in my attic and I heard a clock below strike six. It was already broad daylight, and people had begun to go up and down the stairs. By the door where the wall of the room was papered with old numbers of the Morgenbladet, *I could distinguish clearly a notice from the Director of Lighthouses, and a little to the left of that an inflated advertisement of Fabian Olsen's new-baked bread.*

—opening page of *Hunger*, by Knut Hamsun, Nobel Prize winner

*T*he most common baked goods in the old days were flatbread and *lefse*. Flatbread, a crispy, wafer-thin bread introduced in the 1500s, is a traditional summer side dish in the country. Many villages had an annual communal baking of flatbread. The housewives gathered in a bakehouse. Some mixed the dough while others rolled it out. The dough was rolled very thin and baked over a fire on large stone slabs sprinkled with water. In later years they were baked on gridirons. The flatbread was piled up to eight feet high for winter and stored in the *stabbur*. Flatbread is delicious with *lapskaus* (see page 126).

Popular among fishermen, *lefse* stayed fresh during their long trips at sea. In the autumn women went from house to house to assist in baking *lefse* for the men to take in their "Lofoten Chests." These chests were also a good investment. Only a well-fed, well-clad fisherman could work at such a grueling job during winter. While their men were gone, the women took care of the farms and earned additional income by washing clothes for the crews of the visiting boats or selling waffles, cakes, and *lefse* among the fishing boats. The children earned money by cutting out cod tongues and threading the heads together to ready for drying (see page 72).

❧

Thin Potato Bread

lefse

5 large potatoes, peeled*
½ cup sweet cream
3 tablespoons butter
1 teaspoon salt
½ cup flour per 1 cup mashed potatoes

*You may also use 3 cups prepared instant mashed potatoes. (Choose a brand like Potato Buds that uses potato chunks instead of powder.) Prepare the potatoes according to package instructions. Chill overnight. Mix with 2 tablespoons sugar, 1 tablespoon shortening, and 3 cups all-purpose flour. Knead until smooth.

1. Boil and mash the potatoes. Add cream, butter, and salt. Beat until smooth. Let cool.
2. Add flour, roll into ball, and knead until smooth.
3. Roll out about 1 tablespoon dough on a well-floured surface until your *lefse* is very thin.
4. Cook in an ungreased frying pan over medium-high heat. (Be careful that heat is not too high.) Turn when brown spots appear on *lefse*.
5. Place browned *lefse* between two terrycloth towels or waxed paper to prevent drying. Store in refrigerator or freeze.

Serve with jam, sugar, honey, lingonberries, or wrapped around a hotdog.

MAKES ABOUT 35 *LEFSE*.

❧
Lefse from Numedal

8 ¾ cups whole milk
1¼ cups unsalted butter
1¼ cups lard
4½ pounds (16 cups) wheat flour
2 tablespoons sour cream
2 egg yolks

1. Bring the milk, butter, and lard to a boil.
2. Add the flour, sour cream, and egg yolks. Knead dough well.
3. Cut the dough into golf ball-size pieces. Roll thin. Place between sheets of butter paper until all have been rolled.
4. Fry on a hot griddle, floured side first. Place in cloth to preserve moisture. Butter the *lefse* on the white side and fold in half twice.

Store in a cool place.

MAKES ABOUT **50** *LEFSER.*

The farm at Sevletunet in Numedal boasts one of the best-preserved stabbur *in Norway. When we stopped in one day last September, the proprietor was setting the table for a wedding party which was to take place in the* stabbur. *The building, which dates from 1632—"not including its medieval elements"—is one of the two oldest-preserved barns in Norway. You can rent a room here, complete with bath and kitchen.*

> *H*e hath need of fire, who now is come,
> numbed with cold to the knee;
> food and clothing the wanderer craves
> who has fared o'er the rimy fell.
>
> He craves for water, who comes for refreshment,
> drying and friendly bidding,
> marks of good will, fair fame if 'tis won,
> and welcome once and again.
>
> —*Håvamål*, translated by
> Olive Bray, edited by
> D.L. Ashliman

I am repeatedly delighted by the hospitality we receive on visits in Norway. Once driving back to Oslo from the *hytte* we ran into a roadblock where workers were clearing a small avalanche of stones from the road. My uncle's cousin's farm was located across the river at Hoel just before the road block. We decided to stop in to say hello, hoping that the road would be clear by the time we returned. Within minutes we were at a table decked with homemade *fyrstekake* (see recipe on page 248), delicious brewed coffee, and pancakes baked by Marita (recipe on following page).

Onkel Johnny's grandfather was born nearby at a remote farm in Tveito, so remote, in fact, that every time he paid a courting visit to his girlfriend— who would become Johnny's grandmother—he faced a climb of 1,500 steps up a steep mountain. When they married, they moved to the farm at Hoel, where Johnny's cousin Nils lives today with his wife Marita and their two daughters. Nils moved here to take over the farm when he was 16 years old.

Lappar were traditionally made with a *takke*, a griddle-like instrument used with wood-burning stoves long before the frying pan. The *takke*, which is also used to make flatbread, provides a large cooking surface which gives faster, more even cooking. A cast-iron frying pan will suffice, however.

❧
Marita's Pancakes, or "Patches"

lappar

6 eggs
½ to 1 cup sugar
4½ cups sour milk
2 or 3 teaspoons baking soda
about 6 cups all-purpose flour

1. Whip the eggs and ½ cup sugar together.
2. Add the milk to the baking soda slowly. Mix until smooth. Add to egg mixture. Add flour until you have a thick batter. Add more sugar to taste if necessary.
3. Fry in a *takke*, or cast-iron frying pan until light brown.

Serve cold with blueberries and sugar, jam and sour cream, or *geitost*.

MAKES ABOUT 40 PANCAKES.

❧
Rundstykker

2 cups whole milk, very warm
2 tablespoons (2 packets) yeast
1 teaspoon salt
3 teaspoons sugar
about 5 cups all-purpose flour
1 egg, beaten (optional)

1. Mix milk and yeast together. Add salt and sugar. Add flour slowly until you have a firm and elastic dough. Knead well. Cover and set aside to rise in a warm place, about 45 minutes. Punch down the dough. Set aside to rise again, about 45 minutes.
2. Separate into 25 to 30 rolls. Place on greased cookie sheets. Cover and set aside to rise again, about 15 minutes.
3. Preheat oven to 375° F. If desired, brush the egg over each roll. Bake for 10 to 15 minutes.

MAKES ABOUT 16 ROLLS.

𝔄

*T*his or that, he comes: the figure of a man in this great soli-
tude. He trudges on; bird and beast are silent all about him; now
and again he utters a word or two; speaking to himself. "Eyah—
well, well"—so he speaks to himself. Here and there, where the
moors give place to a kindlier spot, an open space in the midst of
the forest, he lays down the sack and goes exploring . . . He moves
down, and there is a green hillside; far below, a glimpse of the
stream, and a hare bounding across. The man nods his head, as
it were approvingly—the stream is not so broad but that a hare
may cross it at a bound. A white grouse sitting close upon its nest
starts up at his feet with an angry hiss, and he nods again: feath-
ered game and fur—a good spot, this. Heather, bilberry, and
cloudberry cover the ground; there are tiny ferns, and the seven-
pointed star flowers of the wintergreen.

—Excerpted from *Markens Grøde* (*Growth of the Soil*),
   by Knut Hamsun, Winner of Nobel Prize
   for Literature 1920

*E*very October since 1901, the world has watched as Norway hosts the
Nobel prize party. Although Alfred Nobel was a Swede, his 1895 will stipu-
lates that the Storting in Norway present the peace prize. Swedish institu-
tions present the literature and scientific prizes. Perhaps Nobel wanted to
show respect for a country that was united with Sweden until the end of the
nineteenth century. Or perhaps he simply liked Norway. In any case, the
Norwegian Storting appoints five members for the Peace Prize Selection
Committee. The prize has only been awarded seventy times since 1901.

As is evident from Hamsun's words above, bilberries are very common
in Norway's forests. The Norwegians also export the berries to Europe,
where they are used to improve the color of wine.

❧
Pancakes

3 eggs
3 cups whole milk
1¼ cups all-purpose flour
2 tablespoons sugar
½ teaspoon salt
½ teaspoon cardamom
¾ cup bilberries (optional)
butter for frying

1. Mix eggs, milk, flour, sugar, salt, and cardamom together. Knead well. Stir in the bilberries if desired.
2. Melt butter in a frying pan. Spoon about a tablespoon of batter in pan and tilt pan so that batter covers it in a thin layer. Fry until golden brown. Repeat with the rest of the dough.

Serve with jam, fresh berries, or sour cream. An especially popular topping on plain pancakes is blueberry preserves. A light Saturday night supper might consist of tomato soup and pancakes.

MAKES 4 SERVINGS.

🎵

We are still encumbered by so many barbaric Norwegian traditions. True, we are not cannibals—even our worst enemies could not accuse us of so being. But we are drinkers of Aquavit, eaters of brown whey-cheese, and guzzlers of fermented fish!

—*Pictures of Life in the Lion-Salon*, 1848

Today Norway is one of the richest countries in the world, but times were not always so prosperous. In the sixteenth century a string of famines led people to explore options in the kitchen. One culinary secret, for example, was to mix ground tree bark with flour to bake a crude bread called *barkebrød*. I could not find an exact recipe for *barkebrød* to include in these pages, but I can assure you that the bread recipe below is far superior in taste—and certainly as traditionally Norwegian.

The nineteenth century also saw many frugal meals. Culinary expert Hanna Winsnes published a popular pamphlet of the time detailing how families relying on one pig or sheep could use the entire animal, down to the last bone and sinew, for a variety of meals. Other recipes actually called for Icelandic moss and ground animal bones.

The upper class enjoyed such succulent dishes as beef, lamb, grouse, hare, chicken, white bread, even turkey and olives. The Norwegian bourgeois might very well have enjoyed the following traditional bread recipes.

Following is Lisa Anne Yayla's family recipe from Trondheim.

❧
Norwegian Sweet Rolls

boller

about 4½ cups all-purpose flour
1 cup sugar
1 teaspoon salt
1 cup (2 sticks) butter
1½ cups warm whole milk
2 packages fresh yeast
1 egg
1 egg, separated
3 teaspoons cardamom

Preheat oven to 400° F.

1. Sift the flour, sugar, and salt together. Crumble in the butter.
2. Mix 1½ cups warm water and milk. Dissolve the yeast in a little of the warm liquid.
3. Beat the egg and egg yolk together. Mix together to form a dough. Add cardamom. Mix well.
4. Cover and set aside in a warm area for about an hour, or until it has doubled in size. Divide the dough and form small balls, about 3 inches in diameter.
5. Place on greased baking pan. Cover and set aside to rise for 30 to 45 minutes. Beat the egg white with 1 tablespoon cold water. Brush the rolls with the beaten egg white.
6. Bake for about 10 minutes or until golden brown.

MAKES 12 BUNS.

*I*n 1924 in exchange for a studio built especially for him, the sculptor Gustav Vigeland agreed to donate all his works of art to the city of Oslo from that day forward. Today Vigeland's park spreads out over 80 acres and displays 192 sculptural groups in stone, iron, and bronze. The 55-foot-high Monolith, a white granite piece of 36 sculptural groups, dominates the park.

The park boasts several rose gardens, which gained a particular significance during World War II. In those days the industrious people of Oslo grew potatoes in the rose gardens because the soil was so fertile. In fact, when the roses froze in the gardens several years ago, the groundskeepers decided to plant potatoes again to refertilize the soil. In the spring the tourists could be found picking potatoes instead of roses from the garden. Roses were planted again the following year.

A newer rose garden grows on the opposite end of the park. As the story goes, for each of the five years of King Håkon's exile in London, Norwegian commandos returning to Norway on secret missions dug up a fir tree and took it back to the king for Christmas. After the war the people of Oslo continued the custom by sending the tallest tree in their forests to London in thanks to the people of England. In 1953 the people of London sent a rose garden to Oslo to show their appreciation.

℀
Whole Wheat Rolls

1 pound (3½ cups) whole wheat flour, sifted
1 pound (3½ cups) all-purpose flour
2 teaspoons salt
2 teaspoons finely chopped thyme
about ¼ cup dried oatmeal flakes
about 1½ cups water or skim milk
4 tablespoons (4 packets) yeast

1. Mix the flours, salt, thyme, and oatmeal together.
2. Heat the water or milk until it is lukewarm. Mix the yeast into the luke-warm liquid. Add to flour mixture.
3. Knead the dough until it is smooth. If necessary, add more flour until the dough falls away from the edge of the bowl.
4. Cover and set aside to rise, about an hour.
5. Divide the dough into 24 pieces and shape into rolls. Roll each piece in the oatmeal, and place on a greased cookie sheet.
6. Cover and set aside to rise for another 15 to 20 minutes.
7. Preheat oven to 425° F. Bake for 15 minutes.

MAKES 24 ROLLS.

Det trengst ikkje ris, når guten er vis.
No need to spank the lad when he is clever.

*D*uring the Viking age gods and goddesses ruled the earth. Odin, old and wise, ruled over them all. Thor led warriors with his magic hammer. The goddess Freya represented fertility and watched over the soil and livestock. Trickster Loki was a sorcerer not trusted by the other gods.

Like the Vikings the gods ate and drank only between battles. After the Vikings relocated to Iceland, they continued to tell their tales, which today make up one of the richest bodies of work in European medieval literature. The Poetic Edda, The Vinland Saga, and Harald's Saga, a tale of King Harald Hardråda, for example, all survived through oral tradition. Most were written down during the Norwegian Romantic movement.

The Vikings and the Nordmen before them mixed the lives of the gods and the giants with those of Eve's children and elves. Their giants were fond of dropping boulders and islands wherever they chose. Trolls worked in metal and wood and made Thor's hammer. Mischievous elves lived underground. The jotuns, who represented the darker side of life, were everyone's enemies. Much of life took place in the beautiful Jotunheim ("Home of the Giants") mountains in central south Norway, where more than 200 of its many peaks rise above 1900 meters (6233 feet). Today Jotunheim is a popular place to ski or hike.

In the following report Tor Åge Bringsværd explains the lives of the gods.

*H*OW *D*ID THE *W*ORLD *B*EGIN?
by Tor Åge Bringsværd

*I*n the beginning there was Cold and Heat. On one side, *Niflheim*, the land of frost and mist. On the other, *Muspellsheim*, a sea of raging flames. Between them, there was nothing but a vast, bottomless abyss, *Ginnungagap*. Here, in this yawning void—flanked by light and dark—lay the origin of all life. In the encounter between ice and fire . . . slowly the snow began to melt and, shaped by the cold, but brought to life by the heat, a strange creature came into being— a huge troll named *Ymer*. No greater giant has ever lived.

As the ice melted, the drops formed yet another creature—with udders and horns: a colossal cow by the name of *Audhumla*. She had so much milk that it flowed from her huge teats like great rivers. Thus Ymer found food. And Audhumla? She immediately began to lick the salty, frost-covered stones that lay all around the giant and herself. But then something strange occurred. Suddenly the cow licked some long strands of hair from one of the stones! The next day a head and a face appeared from out of the stone. And on the third day the cow finally managed to lick the entire body free. It was a man, tall and handsome. His name was *Bure*, and from him descended the gods, whom we call *Æsir*.

The giant Ymer bore his own child. As he lay sleeping, he began to sweat, and suddenly, from his left armpit, a male and a female emerged. Refusing to be outdone by his arms, Ymer's feet coupled and gave birth to a son with six heads. This was the origin of the Rime Giants, sometimes called trolls, but best known as *Jotuns*.

The various creatures must have managed to live in peace with one another for quite some time. At any rate, they had children together . . . *Odin*—who later became the chief of all the gods—was the son of *Bestla*, daughter of a Jotun, and Bure's son Bor. However, the Rime Giants steadily increased in number and the place was soon swarming with Jotuns. Then one day Odin and his brothers, *Vilje* and *Ve*, rose in revolt against Ymer and his kin. A terrible battle ensued, from which Odin and his brothers emerged victorious. They slew the giant, and a wave of blood flooded over the enemies of the Æsir, drowning them all . . . all but two. From this Jotun couple, who fled into the mist, seeking refuge in the land of fog, descended all the subsequent generations of Rime Giants. Audhumla, the first cow, must also have been washed over the edge of the precipice during the bloodbath, as no one has seen hide nor hair of her ever since. . . . The Æsir dragged Ymer's dead body into the middle of the huge void Ginnungagap, positioning him like a lid over the abyss.

From the body of the giant they then created the world. His blood became the sea, his flesh the land. His knuckles formed cliffs and peaks. His teeth and broken splinters of bone became stones and boulders. His hair turned into trees and grass. The gods threw his brains high into the air, creating clouds. And the sky? That was the giant's skull, which was placed like a vaulted dome over all they had created. Next, the gods caught sparks from the fiery Muspellsheim and hung them in the sky, where they still sparkle brightly. Inside what was once the skull of the giant Ymer ... thus were the stars created.

Small worms crawled out of Ymer's corpse to become the very first dwarfs, who dwelt in the caves and grottoes of the netherworld. The Æsir chose four of the dwarfs to hold up the heavenly vault and guard the four corners of the world. These dwarfs were named *East*, *West*, *North* and *South*.

Thus order and reason came to be.

How was mankind created?

One day, as Odin and his brothers were walking along the beach, they found two wooden logs that had been washed ashore.

They set the logs on end, and brought them to life. Odin blew breath and souls into the logs. Vilje gave them the ability to think and move, while Ve gave them the powers of speech, hearing and sight. The gods infused them with warmth and color. No longer mere driftwood, the logs had become Man and Woman. The Æsir called the man *Ask* and the woman *Embla*, from whom all human beings are descended.

How did time begin?

In the beginning there was no time. Everything stood strangely still.

However, the Æsir gave the Jotun woman *Night* and her son *Day* a horse and carriage each, placing them in the sky, where they were to circle the world every day. Night rode in front, mounted on her steed *Rimfakse*. Its mane was silver with frost, and the dew that fell on the fields every morning were drops of foam from the horse's bit. Night was followed by her son Day. His horse was named *Skinfakse* because of its gleaming mane.

The gods then took sparks from Muspellsheim to make the sun and set the moon on its proper course. Each of them was given a celestial chariot, with two children to ensure that they did not fall off and to drive the swift horses. The sun and the moon sped across the sky, constantly pursued by two huge wolves that snapped at their heels, trying to devour them! And one day . . . one day perhaps they will succeed. . . .

Was their world round?

It was round—but not like an apple or a ball. The world was circular in shape . . . like a thin, flat slice of wood sawn off the end of a log.

Where in the world did we and the Æsir live?

In the beginning everything was jungle or desert. But like pioneers, the Æsir cleared the land, creating a space to live in, both for themselves and for us. They called mankind's home *Midgard* because it was situated in the middle of the world. In the center of Midgard—so that men and women would not feel alone and abandoned—the gods built a stronghold for themselves named *Åsgard*, a gigantic fortress surrounded by thick walls. The fortress could only be entered by riding over the rainbow, a fiery bridge of flames. Strong bulwarks were also erected around Midgard to protect it from the dark and terrible forces that reigned in the wild, uncharted terrain outside the walls. There, in *Utgard* and *Jotunheim*, lived the Jotuns and trolls. Thus the world was structured like the rings of a tree trunk. All around, on every side, the mighty ocean lapped at its edge.

But weren't there dwarfs and elves in the world too?

Yes, there were elves and dwarfs. Dwarfs were usually to be found among rocks and cliffs, often hidden away underground in Midgard and Utgard. Although they were skillful smiths, they were never fully to be trusted. Elves, on the other hand, were friends to both gods and men. They lived in *Alvheim*, which was believed by some to be located within the walls of Åsgard and by others in Midgard. So little is known about dwarfs and elves. Some people even believe them to be related and that they should be called "light elves" and "dark elves." At one time, there was another race of gods besides the Æsir who were called the Vanar and who lived in *Vanaheim*. However, their fortress was destroyed and now no mortal knows where its site lay. . . .

Did the world have a center?

At the center of Midgard lay Åsgard. At the center of Åsgard the gods planted a tree, a mighty ash called *Yggdrasil*. It was the largest tree imaginable. One of its roots lay in Åsgard, another in Jotunheim and a third in Niflheim. Its branches were so widespread that they embraced the entire world. Yggdrasil was the center of the world. As long as the tree remained green and lush and put forth new shoots, the world would continue to exist.

Who could see the future? Who knew what fate would bring?

Three goddesses of destiny—the *Norns* Urd, Verdande and Skuld—dwelt beside a well in Åsgard. The Norns knew the destiny of every living being and what lay in store for everyone and everything. Some people maintain that there were other Norns as well, among the elves and dwarfs. Among human beings, too, there were women who could see more than others. This kind of soothsayer was called a *Volve*, which means "stave-bearer." Her stave was the symbol of her supernatural powers. By entering into a trance, she could contact the spiritual world, and she knew many powerful magic spells.

Who were the most important gods?

Odin was the greatest of the gods. A sage and magician, he ruled over all the gods. Wednesday is his day (Odin's day), while Friday is named after his wife *Frigg* (Frigg's day). Odin's horse Sleipner had eight legs. Odin also had two ravens (Hugin and Munin), who flew out over the world every morning to watch and listen, returning home in the evening to report to Odin all they had seen. His spear Gungnir never failed to hit its mark. From his ring Draupne, eight rings of equal magnificence dripped every ninth night. Odin had only one eye; as a young man, he had pawned the other to the giant *Mime* for the right to drink from the marvelous fountain of wisdom guarded by the giant. (Mime was later beheaded, but Odin found the giant's bloody skull and anointed it with healing herbs. The eyes in the head immediately opened and the mouth was again able to form words. After that, Mime's head remained one of Odin's most cherished advisers.)

Odin's son *Thor* was the second mightiest god. Thursday (Thor's day) is his day. Strong and quick-tempered, Thor was always ready to do battle with giants and trolls. Although *Tyr* (Tuesday—Tyr's day) might have been a little braver, no one in the whole world was as strong as Thor. His hammer Miolnir was the most dangerous weapon, both in heaven and on earth. Thor could make it as small or as large as he wanted. When he threw it, it always struck its target and then returned to his hand. Whenever he travelled, his chariot was drawn by goats instead of horses. His goats, Cracktooth and Gaptooth, could be slaughtered in the evening and yet be full of life again the next morning, if care was taken not to break a single bone when eating the goatmeat, and if all the bones were collected and placed in the goatskins at the end of the meal. Thunder was the sound made by Thor's chariot rolling across the sky.

Siv was the name of Thor's wife. Her hair was made of pure gold, and of all the goddesses only *Freya*—the goddess of love—was more beautiful. Freya was also the one who taught the Æsir the art of witchcraft. She owned a magic feather cloak, with which she could transform herself into a falcon whenever she desired, and she drove a chariot drawn by cats. Although everyone turned to Freya for assistance or consolation in matters of the heart, she was unable to heal her own eternally broken heart. Her husband had left her to wander the world (no one knew where). Freya often wept bitterly over her loss, and her tears were of the purest gold. Freya's brother was named *Frey*, which means "Lord" or "The Foremost One." Frey was the god of fertility. Both he and Freya were actually descended from the Vanir (the race of gods against whom the Æsir fought for control of the world at the beginning of time). Along with their aged father the two children had originally come to the Æsir as hostages. Frey owned a magic boar named Goldenbristle, which could run as fast on land as on sea and in the air. He also possessed the magic ship Skidblaner, whose sails were always filled with wind and which could be folded up like a piece of cloth and put away in his pouch when he wasn't using it. The gods in Åsgard had many other priceless treasures, but the finest of them all were the magic apples tended by the goddess *Idunn*—the apples of youth that the gods had to take a bite of from time to time to avoid growing old and decrepit.

Odin had many sons. Although it is impossible to mention all of them, we cannot get around *Heimdall.* Nor could anyone else! Heimdall, who was born in a miraculous manner of nine young giant girls way back at the dawn of time, was the watchman of the gods. He lived near Himmelberget and stood guard over the rainbow bridge Bifrost. Heimdall needed less sleep than a bird, could see as clearly by night as by day and could hear the grass grow. He owned the Giallar Horn, which he was to blow on the very last day to summon the Æsir to arms in the final great battle against trolls and the powers of darkness.

Balder, the son of Odin and Frigg, was renowned for his friendliness, gentleness and wisdom. Balder was haunted by nightmares and was afraid of dying, but his mother—the most powerful of all the Åsgard goddesses—extracted an oath from everyone and everything that no one would ever do him harm. The gods soon made a game of flinging weapons at Balder, since he could no longer be killed or wounded. However, Frigg forgot to ask the mistletoe, which she considered too small and insignificant. Loki the Troublemaker learned of this, and deceived the blind Hod into killing Balder with an arrow made of mistletoe. The Æsir sent a rider to Helheim, the Realm of the Dead, to ask for Balder's return. Hel, Queen of Helheim, replied that Balder would be restored to life if the entire world shed tears over his fate. And everything and everyone—even the stones and trees—are still trying to weep the dead god back to life in vain.

Who were the enemies of the gods and humans?

Although sometimes known as Rime Giants or Trolls, they generally went by the name of Jotuns. These giants lived in the wilderness and rugged mountains of Utgard and Jotunheim. Often huge and mighty hulks, they were forces of chaos. The only Æsir who could really hold his own with them in a wrestling match was Thor, the God of Thunder. However, the Jotuns had unrivalled magic powers. On one occasion, for example, they fashioned a huge giant out of clay, and called him *Mokkurkalve*. An artificial, living being that was terrible to behold—ninety kilometers tall and with a chest span of thirty kilometers! Jotun giantesses rode on wolves, using vipers for reins. While they could be frightfully ugly and some truly monstrous, they could also be incredibly beautiful . . . so lovely that even Odin on more than one occasion allowed himself to be lured into wild, amorous adventures.

Weren't Loki and his children even more dangerous?

A troublemaker and schemer, Loki was originally a Jotun. However, at an early age he mixed blood with Odin and was therefore accepted among the Æsir.

Loki was a joker, a trait that eventually led to his downfall. He betrayed the Æsir and caused the death of Balder. As punishment for this heinous act, he was chained beneath a serpent that dripped deadly, acid venom onto his face. However, his wife *Sigyn*, who remained loyal to him, stood patiently by his side holding a large bowl to catch the poisonous venom. From time to time, however, she had to turn aside to empty the bowl. Then the venom dripped right onto Loki's face, making him writhe so violently that the entire world trembled. This is what is called earthquakes. Loki had children in Åsgard, as well as other, stranger offspring. With the giantess *Angerboda*, he fathered the *Fenris Wolf,* the *Midgard Serpent* and *Hel,* and he gave birth to the horse *Sleipner,* after coupling with the stallion Svadilfare.

The *Fenris Wolf,* a truly monstrous beast, grew up in Åsgard, but soon became so huge, wild and dangerous that only the god Tyr dared to feed it. The Æsir had the dwarfs forge an unbreakable chain, Gleipnir, which was made of the sound of a cat's footfall, the beard of a woman, the roots of a rock, the sinews of a bear, the breath of a fish and the spittle of a bird. (That is why a cat's footfall no longer makes any sound, why women have no beard, etc.) By great cunning they managed to tie the wolf up so tightly that it could barely move, and thrust a sword into its mouth so that its jaws were always open yet unable to bite. It is only when the world comes to an end that it will finally be able to shake off its bonds. . . .

The second child that Loki conceived with the giantess Angerboda was a serpent. The Æsir threw it into the sea, where it eventually grew so incredibly large that they called it the *Midgard Serpent* because it encircled the entire earth, holding its own tail in its mouth.

Nonetheless, it is perhaps the last of Loki and Angerboda's three children who has caused the most trouble for Æsirs and mortals. She was a ghastly girlchild, half black, half white. She was expelled from Åsgard and settled far to the north, where she created a subterranean realm of the dead, a cold, damp, gray world. Her name, and that of the kingdom over which she ruled, was *Hel.* All those who died of illness and old age went to Hel, where they led a sad, shadowy existence. The Queen of Death herself resembled a corpse, and everything she owned had names reminiscent of the cold "life" in the grave. In the olden days, when people felt the presence of ghosts, they would say, "The gate to Hel is open." On the day of the Last Great Battle, Hel and her army of dead will do battle with the Æsir.

Were there any other places to go after death?

Those who displayed valor on the battlefield went to Odin or Freya when they died. The king of the gods sent out Valkyries clad in coats of mail to fetch fallen heroes. These female warriors were armed and could ride through the air. In Åsgard the dead were divided up between Odin and Freya. Half of them lived with Odin in *Valhall* ("val" means battlefield), and the other half with Freya in *Folkvang* ("folk" in this context meaning men arrayed for battle).

While little is known about life in Folkvang, there are numerous descriptions of Valhalla. On the embankment outside the enormous "barracks," the heroes were allowed to fight to their heart's content all day long. It did not matter if they lost an arm or two because in the evening they arose from the battlefield without a scratch. As friends on the best of terms, they marched into the vast banquet hall where beautiful Valkyries served them mead and boiled pork. *Sæhrimnir*, the pig they ate, was also unique. Every day it was slaughtered and eaten, yet when dawn came it had been restored to life.

On the final day Odin will lead the Æsir and the dead heroes in the last great battle against the Jotuns and the powers of darkness. He himself will fight the Fenris Wolf and will be devoured by the monster. All this has been prophesied.

Can gods die?

Yes, gods can die.

How will the world end?

As the end draws nigh, there will be famine and strife. This final period is called *Ragnarok*, which means "the twilight of the gods." Brother will slay brother and son will not spare his own father. Three continuous years of *Fimbul* winter will then ensue, after which sky-wolves will devour the sun and the moon. Mountains will crumble, and every bond will be broken. The *Fenris Wolf* will finally be loosed and will run around the world with jaws agape. Its lower jaw will drag along the ground, its upper jaw will touch the clouds. Its eyes will burn with a strange fire, and its nostrils will breathe flames. *Loki* will be freed. He will rig a ghastly vessel, *Naglfar*, a ship made of dead men's nails. With ragged sails and a crew of rotting corpses, he will sail up from his daughter's realm of the dead. The *Midgard serpent* will slither ashore, winding its way over fields and meadows. To the south the heavens will be torn asunder. From the country beyond—the frightening, unknown Muspellsheim, land of fire that existed long before Odin and his brothers created the world—will come a mighty host of riders clad in shining vestments, armed with fiery swords. As they charge forward everything will burst into flame and burn, and the great rainbow bridge will collapse under their weight. The final, decisive and bloody battle will be fought at a place called the Plain of Vigrid (a thousand kilometers wide and a thousand kilometers long). Odin will be devoured by the Fenris Wolf. Thor and the Midgard Serpent will slay each other, as will Heimdall and Loki. The whole world will go up in flames. Even Yggdrasil—the great world tree—will burn. When the flames die down, the world will be a smoking ruin. The charred remains will sink below the surface of the sea and disappear.

Will that be the end?

No. Out of the sea a new earth, green and lovely, will grow, fertile as a dream, with fields that sow themselves, and an abundance of fish and game. No one will go hungry any more, nor will anyone suffer from the cold. Behold! The sun has given birth to a daughter. An end has been put to all evil. The earth has been washed clean. A new life may begin! Åsgard is no more. Not a single stone remains of the old fortress of the gods. Nonetheless, it is to Åsgard that the Æsir who were not slain in the last, great battle will return.

So someone will survive?

The fortunate—those who shall inherit the earth.

Are there any mortals among them?

Just one man and one woman survive. Their names are *Lif* and *Lifthrasir*. They sought refuge in a place called Hoddminir's Holt and thus escaped the conflagration. They are disgorged, alive, by the sea. The morning dew is long their only food. From these two mortals a new human race will arise.

So there is hope after all?

According to the myths, there will *always* be hope.

—Excerpted from *Information: Norway:* "Norse Mythology,"
produced for the Ministry of Foreign Affairs

*U*llensvang, one of the gems of the Hardanger region, takes its name from the Old Norse god Ull, the god of skiing and hunting. The parson of Ullensvang can be credited for the area's great popularity among travelers. At the beginning of the nineteenth century, parson Niels Hertzberg was the only person in the district who could speak English and French. When foreigners visited the area, he would often house them, feed them, and relay glowing details of his parish. Indeed, the parsonage was the first inn of the district.

To encourage more visitors to the area, Hertzberg also prepared the first brochure of his parish Lofthus and the Hardanger region. Sixteenth-century Lofthus originated on the farm Opedal, which took its name from the Opo River. After the death of one of its owners, the farm was divided between two heirs. Modern buildings with a loft were erected on the new farm, hence the name Lofthus. Today the whole village (population 800) is called Lofthus. In addition to acting as its first tour guide, Hertzberg also imported the potato and the sweet cherry to the district and taught farmers how to graft fruit trees, an art that had disappeared with the monks.

The following recipe is the specialty of Bent Larsen, the chef at Hotel Ullensvang. Established in 1846, the hotel is still family owned. Its founder Hans Utne was 14 years old when he rowed across the fjord from Utne. He came from a family of 14 brothers and sisters who lived on a croft too small to sustain such a large family. Hans moved out and built a boathouse on a small piece of land on the opposite banks of the fjord. Many visitors to the area came by sea, and, like the parson, Hans Utne offered guests his own straw bed in the loft over the shipping office for accommodation. After one year he expanded his facilities by 100% by providing a second bed. The foundations for Hotel Ullensvang were laid.

Requirements to operate a guesthouse were different then. His license read: "For the well-being and relaxation of the visitor, spirits shall be available in the establishment at all hours, so the traveler may refresh himself with a drink." In other words, in those days a hotel owner was required to keep a stock of spirits at all times!

Chef Bent Larsen warns that *komler* is a heavy, salty meal. In Ullensvang *komler* are traditionally served on Thursdays. One local restaurant even has a custom-made serving dish for *komler*, including a bowl in the middle for the bacon butter. Around the edge of the dish the potter wrote: "Dear God: Please give us *komler* every Thursday when we come to heaven as well."

❧

Norwegian Potato Dumplings

komler

3½ cups peeled raw potatoes
1 to 2 potatoes, peeled and boiled
2 tablespoons barley flour
2 tablespoons wheat flour
1 teaspoon salt

1. Grind or grate the raw potatoes. Cut the boiled potatoes into small pieces.
2. Mix with flours and salt. Knead well.
3. Shape the mixture into large egg-size balls. Poach in boiling salted water for about 25 minutes. Set aside in the same water until ready to serve.

Serve with rutabaga, salted and smoked lamb, smoked beef sausages, sausages, and bacon butter.

MAKES 4 SERVINGS.

❧
Potato Dumplings II

2 pounds (about 6 medium) potatoes
1 cup barley meal
1 cup finely ground whole meal flour
4 teaspoons salt

1. Peel and shred the potatoes. Squeeze the moisture out of the potatoes. Mash well. Stir in meal, flour, and 1 teaspoon salt.
2. Add the 3 teaspoons salt to 4 cups water and bring to a boil. Shape the potatoes into egg-size dumplings and lower them carefully into the boiling water. Simmer for 45 minutes.

MAKES 4 SERVINGS.

We discovered the tiny hamlet of Hjølmo on a drive around the Hardanger region. This picturesque scene of a handful of homes nestled in a valley evokes a sense of timelessness. Until recently, residents lived here year-round. We met one resident currently employed on an oil platform on the North Sea who was born in this house. As a boy, he would walk 5 kilometers (3 miles) to school every day. When he did not feel like going to school, he would tell his parents that there had been an avalanche and he had to return home.

As you can see from the picture of this house in Hjølmo, Norwegians often use sheep and goats to cut the grass on the roof.

Υou will find *pølser og lomper* (hotdogs and *lomper*) for sale on every street corner in every major city in Norway. It is a wonderful variation to the hotdog bun, and the Norwegians eat it like you would a hotdog—with mustard, ketchup, and (pickled) relish.

℘
Potato Cakes

lomper

about 3 pounds (about 9 medium) boiled potatoes, mashed
1 cup all-purpose white flour
pinch of salt

1. Mix potatoes, flour, and salt together until smooth.
2. Place 1 tablespoon of mixture on a hot frying pan or electric burner. Fry until a golden brown. Flip occasionally to prevent burning.

Serve with hot dogs, butter, and jam, or with sugar and cinnamon.

MAKES ABOUT 15 SERVINGS.

Desserts

*O*nly about 3% of Norway is developed or arable land. The rest of the country claims a spectacular assortment of moss, forest, and berry bushes. Blueberries, wild scarlet currants, and the high mountain cloudberry, which looks like an orange blackberry, are just a few of the berry bushes that tempt hikers to climb around the nooks and crannies of Norway's rocky hills. Berry picking is in fact so popular that many places in the countryside offer berry-picking holidays.

According to law, you are free to pick every berry in the countryside except for the cloudberries of Nordland, Troms, and Finnmark. They are protected because many residents gather them for income. By law, the landowners have the rights to them. The cloudberry contains natural preservatives and keeps without being treated in any way. It is considered an excellent source of vitamin C in winter.

Cloudberries have a delicate taste, and the following dessert is the perfect way to serve them. I tasted this delicious dish last summer at the *hytte* in Hardanger.

❧

Cloudberry Cream

multer

1 cup cloudberries
¼ to ½ cup sugar
1½ cups whipped cream

1. Mix the cloudberries with sugar.
2. Fold into the whipped cream.

MAKES 2 SERVINGS.

⚭
Onkel Johnny's Skipperkake *(skipper's cake)*

1 cup sugar
3 eggs
1 cup butter
¾ cup all-purpose flour
1½ teaspoon baking powder
½ to ¾ cup ground almonds
6 or 7 ounces Hershey's special dark mildly sweet chocolate, grated
confectioners' sugar

Preheat oven to 325° F.

1. Whisk the sugar and eggs together.
2. Blend in the butter, flour, baking powder, almonds, and chocolate together. Do not melt the butter before mixing. Place dough in a 9 × 12-inch pan.
3. Bake for 45 minutes on the lowest ring of the oven. Remove and cool.

Sprinkle confectioners' sugar over cake before serving.

MAKES 12 TO 16 SERVINGS.

𝔚𝔈

𝒲here will you find the good, the fine,
the great to grow in chains?
Parch the meadow—no grass grows green;
bind the eagle, and on its crag it dies;
stem the source, that has set out
merrily on its tour,
and all you have is a poisonous swamp!
Nature, strong and free,
hates all chains.

—Henrik Wergeland from
Milestones of Norwegian Literature

𝒯he Hardanger hills, which are popular among Norwegians, are the orchards of Norway. Apples, pears, plums and even cherries grow around the family *hytte* in these hills. Following are two special favorites made from Hardanger berries.

𝔈𝔈

Raspberry Dessert

bringebær dessert

𝒮tores like Haram-Christensen Corp. listed at the end of the book carry such specialty items as the vanilla sauce called for below.

1 cup raspberries
½ cup vanilla sauce

1. Place berries in a dessert bowl. Pour the vanilla sauce over the berries.
2. Place plate under the grill or in oven for a few minutes or until the surface of the sauce is golden brown.

Serve immediately.

MAKES 1 SERVING.

*I*n my dream on the mountain
Below the rushing waterfall,
A fairy gave me her harp

—*J. S. Welhaven*

The fiddle-playing fossegrim *lives in waterfalls. Aspiring fiddle players often visit him there and offer food in exchange for fiddle lessons. If the food offered is inadequate,* fossegrimen *will only teach the fiddler to tune his instrument, not how to play it.*

The "seven sisters," seven waterfalls, fall just opposite the "suitor" waterfall (above) in the Geirangerfjord. The suitor asked all seven sisters, one after the other, to marry him. All refused. Discouraged, the suitor began to drink. Do you see the bottle?

⅋

Kringle

*K*ringle is often served for tea.

1 stick margarine
1¼ cups all-purpose flour
4 eggs

ICING

confectioners' sugar
juice from ½ lemon

Preheat oven to 350° F.

1. Bring margarine and 9 ounces water to a boil. Remove from heat and add flour. Stir until very well blended. Set aside to cool.
2. Add eggs to mixture one at a time, mixing well.
3. Spoon dough onto a greased cookie sheet. Form into the shape of a figure eight.
4. Bake on second rack from bottom of oven for about 40 minutes or until golden brown. Wait the entire 40 minutes before opening oven or the cake will fall.
5. Combine confectioners' sugar and lemon juice to make icing. Remove cake from oven. Spread icing on the cake.

MAKES 8 TO 10 SERVINGS.

> N*orwegians are very clever people. They know that trolls do not exist. The question is, do the trolls know?*
>
> —Old Norwegian saying

Trolls have lived in Norway for thousands of years. They come in all sizes. Some have one head, others have five. Some are as big as a mountain, others are as small as a grouse. Some, like the *huldrefolk,* live only in the underworld, while *bergfolk* live in the mountains, the *haugfolk* in the hills, and the *underjordiske* live below ground. *Haugfolket* are envious of the people who are able to live out in the sunlight (*i solheimen*). Although they are smaller than humans, their world is much like our world and most are farmers and fishermen. Only the *huldre*-people can enter into our world; many *huldre*-girls seduce men and take them underground to live. (*Hulder* is defined as an alluring siren with a cow's tail.) You can often tell where a troll has been by marks in the landscape. A giant left the Giant Cut Jutulhogget, for example, which is situated in the Østerdal valley in Eastern Norway.

Legend has it that these people are the descendants of the children that Eve hid from God. When He discovered that they had been hidden, God proclaimed that what had once been hidden should remain hidden and assigned them regions in which to live. Others say that they are the angels that the Lord expelled from paradise.

As recent as the eighteenth century, villagers would ring the church bells to drive trolls away, although today Norwegians have learned to cohabit with them comfortably. They've even been known to name areas and activities affectionately for trolls. The annual giant slalom held at Trollstigen, for example, which lies under 20-foot-deep snowbanks even in June, is called the "Troll Ski Race." The Troll train travels from Måbø Valley and the Vøring waterfall in Eidfjord. And the 3,300-foot Troll Wall near Trondheim is the highest vertical mountain wall in Europe. Be careful if you call someone *trolsk* "trollish"; it can still carry connotations like sly, small-minded, or spiteful.

Even the following dessert is named for the trolls. *Norway's Delight* provided the following recipe. It's magic cream: the more you whip it, the more fluff you get!

❧
Magic Cream
trollkrem

3 egg whites
3 tablespoons sugar
juice of ½ lemon
1 cup applesauce

1. Beat egg whites until stiff. Add sugar and lemon juice. Whip until fluffy.
2. Add applesauce.

MAKES 6 SERVINGS.

The guest of honor at the 1994 Olympic Games at Lillehammer. Lillehammer's coat of arms depicts the famous Birkebeiners, or Birchlegs, who became national heroes when they rescued the two-year-old Prince Håkon Håkonsen from pursuers in 1206. Called Birchlegs because of footwear made from animal skins wrapped around birch bark, those brave Nordmen carried the young prince over the mountains from Lille-hammer to Østerdal and safety. Their famous flight is commemorated in an annual March Birkebeiner ski race, which covers the 55 kilome-ters (34 miles) between Lillehammer and Rena. More than 6,000 competitors ski—carrying a 3.5-kilo (8-pound) backpack to represent the child saved by the Birchlegs.

Nicknamed the Athens of Norway, Lillehammer is popular among artists for its spe-cial light. The town's Stågata (Stand Street), which the whole world got to know during the Winter Games, has received the national prize for civic architecture. Visit the Norges Olympiske Museum, housed in one of the arenas built for the 1994 Olympics. The city's Maihaugen open-air museum is also worth a visit, as is Hunderfossen Lekeland, just outside the city. The massive troll here hides a huge grotto that displays Norwegian folk characters. Finally, take the Skibladner, the world's oldest paddle steamer still in opera-tion, which floats on Lillehammer's Lake Mjosa. My mother and her brother and sister enjoyed their childhood summers here. They stayed in nearby Biri, not far from my great grandmother's birthplace.

Askelad and the Silver Ducks

There once was a poor man who had three sons. When he died, the two eldest sons went out into the world to make their fortune, but they would not let the youngest son go with them. "We know what you're fit for!" they said. "All you do is squat by the fire, fiddling with the ashes."

"I'll go alone, then," said Askelad.

The two eldest brothers walked off and made their way to the king's farm. There they entered into service, one under the stable groom and one under the gardener. Askelad started out too and took with him a big kneading-trough, the only thing their parent had left them. The other brothers had not cared about it and it was heavy to carry, but he did not like to leave it behind. After walking a while, he also came to the king's farm and asked for service. They told him they did not need him. Still he kept asking so politely that in the end he was allowed to help in the kitchen and carry wood and water for the cook. He was quick and willing to work, and soon he was well liked by everyone there. But the two other brothers were lazy and got blows by the dozen and little wages. And they grew envious of Askelad when they saw him doing so well.

Opposite the king's farm, on the other side of a big lake, there lived a troll who had seven silver ducks. These ducks basked and swam on the lake and they could be seen from the king's farm. The king had often wished they were his, and one day the two eldest brothers said to the groom, "If our brother liked, he could easily get the seven silver ducks for the king. He has said so." And you can be sure the groom lost no time in passing this on to the king.

Then the king called in Askelad and said to him, "Your brothers tell me you are willing to get me those silver ducks. Go and get them now."

"I've never thought of such a thing," said the lad.

But the king was not to be put off. "You've said you'll do it," he said, "and I'm going to take you at your word, my lad."

"Well," said the lad, "if there's no way out of it, please let me have a quarter of rye and a quarter of wheat, and I'll try and get them." He was given the rye and the wheat and he stored it in the kneading-trough he had brought from home, and in this he rowed across the lake. After he reached the other side, he walked along the shore scattering the grain. At last he was able to lure the ducks inside his trough, and then he rowed back as fast as he could.

When he got to the middle of the lake, the troll came out and saw him.

"Have you made off with my seven silver ducks?" he shouted.

"I have," said the lad.

"Will you be coming again?" asked the troll.

"I might," said the lad.

When he came back to the king with the seven silver ducks, he became even more popular in the household and the king himself gave him praise. But his brothers grew more sullen and jealous, and they decided to tell the groom that Askelad had said he could get the king the troll's quilt with all the checks of silver and gold, any time at all. And the groom wasted no time in telling the king this news. Then the king spoke to the lad, and told him he knew from his brothers that he had boasted of being able to get hold of the troll's quilt with the silver and gold checks. Now he was to do so, or pay with his life. Askelad replied that he had never said any such thing. But it was no use, and so he asked for three days to find a plan. Three days later, he rowed across the lake again in his kneading-trough and walked about keeping careful watch. At last he caught sight of the hill folk putting out the quilt to air it. And as soon as they disappeared inside the mountain, Askelad seized the quilt and rowed back as fast as he could.

When he was out in the middle of the lake, the troll came long and saw him.

"Didn't you steal my seven silver ducks?" shouted the troll.

"Yes, I did," said the lad.

"And have you just stolen my quilt with all the checks of silver and gold?"

"I have," said the lad.

"Will you be coming here again?"

"I might," said the lad.

When he returned with the gold and silver quilt, he became even more popular, and he was made the king's personal servant. This made the other brothers much more vexed, and in revenge they agreed to say to the groom, "Our brother has told us that he can get the king the troll's golden harp. This harp makes everyone glad when they hear it, no matter how sad they are."

And the groom went straight to the king and told him the news, and the king said to the lad, "I'm going to take you at your word again. If you get me the harp, I'll give you my daughter and half my kingdom. If you don't, you'll pay with your life."

"I've never thought or said any such thing," replied Askelad. "But I suppose there's no choice and I'd better try. Could you let me have six days to find a plan?" The six days were granted and when they were over he had to set out. He took with him in his pocket a nail, a birch-twig, and a candle-end, and rowed across the lake. Near the mountain he started pacing quickly to and fro. And after a while the troll came out and saw him.

"Didn't you steal my seven silver ducks?" shouted the troll.

"I did," said the lad.

"And didn't you steal my quilt with the silver and gold checks as well?"

"Yes, I did," said the lad.

Then the troll seized him and carried him inside the mountain. "Well, daughter," he said. "Now I've caught the boy who stole my silver ducks and my quilt with the checks of silver and gold. Fatten him up and we can kill him and invite our friends to a feast." She set to work at once and put him in the fattening pen. And he was there for eight days, and was given the best food and drink, as much as he wanted.

After eight days had passed, the troll told his daughter to go and cut his little finger to find out whether he was fat enough.

She went down to the fattening pen. "Give me your little finger," she said. But Askelad offered her the nail he had brought with him and she cut that.

"Oh, he's still as hard as nails," said the troll's daughter when she came in to her father. "He's not ready yet."

Eight days later the same thing happened, only this time Askelad held out the birch twig. "He's a bit better," she said when she came back to her father. "But he's still as tough as wood."

But after eight days more, the troll told his daughter to go out again and see whether he as fat enough yet. "Give me your little finger," said the troll's daughter to Askelad in the fattening pen. And this time he let her have the candle-end.

"I think he's fair enough now," she said.

"Oh, is he?" said the troll. "I'll be off then and invite our guests. In the meantime you can kill him and roast one half of him and boil the other."

After the troll had gone, the daughter began to sharpen a long, long knife.

"Are you going to use that to slaughter me?" asked the lad.

"Yes, my lad!" said the troll's daughter.

"But the blade's not keen enough," said the lad. "I can sharpen it for you, and then it will be all the easier for you to kill me."

And she gave him the knife, and he started to whet the blade.

"Let me try it on your hair," said the lad. "It should be just right now." And she let him do so. But as he took her by the hair he bent back her neck and cut off her head. Then he boiled half of her and roasted the other half and set the dish on the table. And he dressed himself in her clothes and sat down in a far corner.

When the troll came home with his guests, he thought it was his daughter sitting there and asked her to come and join them at their meal.

"No," answered the lad. "I don't want anything to eat. I feel out of sorts."

"Well, you know how to raise your spirits," said the troll. "Play upon our golden harp."

"Oh yes! Where is it again?" asked Askelad.

"You know well enough. You had it last. It's hanging up there over the door!" said the troll.

Askelad did not need to be told twice. He took down the harp and wandered in and out playing upon it. But all of a sudden he pushed his kneading-trough out on the lake and rowed off so fast that the waters swirled about him.

After a while the troll thought his daughter had been away a long time and he went out to see what was the matter. Then he caught sight of the lad in his trough far out in the middle of the lake.

"Aren't you the one who stole my seven ducks?" shouted the troll.

"Yes," said Askelad.

"And didn't you steal my quilt with the silver and gold checks as well?"

"Yes," said Askelad.

"Have you just taken my golden harp?" cried the troll.

"Yes, I have," said the lad.

"Haven't I eaten you up, then?"

"No! You've eaten your daughter," answered the lad.

And when the troll heard this, he became so angry that he burst. So then Askelad rowed back to the mountain and carried away a heap of gold and silver, as much as he could store in his trough. After he returned to the king's farm with the golden harp, he wedded the princess and got half the kingdom, just as the king had promised. But he was good to his brothers, for he believed that they had only meant well when they spoke of him in the household.

*Askelad, "ash-lad," is the Norwegian version of Cinderella, "little cinder girl."

—Excerpted with permission from
A Time for Trolls, Fairy Tales from Norway

❧
Turi's Ice Cream

is

12 egg yolks
1 cup confectioners' sugar
4⅓ cups whipping cream
instant coffee or cognac (optional)

1. Whip the egg yolks and the sugar together. Add whipping cream to taste. Turi recommends adding a bit of instant coffee or cognac for more taste.
2. You can vary the sweetness by adding more or less sugar. Turi also uses slightly less cream sometimes for a stronger taste.
3. Place in desired form. Freeze immediately.

MAKES 6 TO 8 SERVINGS.

Everybody loves is.

❧

Cream Cake or Layer Cake
bløtkake

*M*y mormor's *bløtkake* tastes especially delicious when made from the berries of Hardanger. I've celebrated my birthday with this cake for as long as I can remember.

4 eggs
1 cup sugar
1 heaping tablespoon potato flour (substitute: cornstarch. Potato flour
    gives a good texture to cake.)
1 cup self-rising flour

FILLING

1 cup sliced peaches with juice, canned pineapple, frozen raspberries, or
    raspberry jam (any fruit of your choice)
1½ cups whipping cream
sugar to taste

1. Whip the eggs and sugar together. Sift the flours together and fold into egg mixture. Carefully mix.
2. Pour the batter into a greased round spring pan.
3. Do not preheat oven. Bake at 350° F for 35 to 40 minutes. Set aside on a rack to cool.
4. Slice cake into two or three parts, horizontally. Sprinkle each part with juices from fruit. Cover one or, if you have three layers, two of the layers with fruit.
5. Whip the cream with the sugar. Cover the fruit with cream, saving most of the cream for the outside of the cake. Place one layer on top of the other. Top with the layer that has no fruit. Cover the whole cake with the rest of the whipped cream.

Garnish with berries or fruit.

MAKES 12 TO 14 SERVINGS.

⅋⅋

Smørkrem

*T*his is another popular filling for *bløtkake.*

¾ cup margarine
1¾ cups confectioners' sugar
½ square baking chocolate
2 tablespoons coffee
1 or 2 teaspoons rum essence

1. Mix all ingredients together well.
2. Add more coffee or rum if desired.

Mormor knitting in Kragerø.

❧
Strawberries and Cream

jordbær og krem

This is my favorite dessert in the world. It makes me dream of Norway in the summer. *Jordbær,* which means "earth-berry," grows all over Norway.

1 pound fresh strawberries
about 1 cup cream or whole milk
sugar

1. Hull the strawberries. Wash them. Drain in a colander.
2. Serve with cream or milk. Sprinkle sugar liberally over them.

MAKES 4 TO 6 SERVINGS.

❧
Cinnamon Wheels

½ cup (1 stick) butter
1¾ cup whole milk
4 tablespoons (4 packets) yeast
6 tablespoons sugar
about 4 cups all-purpose flour

FILLING

5 tablespoons butter, softened
5 tablespoons sugar
1 tablespoon cinnamon
1 egg, beaten

1. Melt the butter over low heat. Add milk, stirring slowly. Add yeast, stirring until it dissolves.
2. Mix in sugar and flour. Knead until dough is firm. Cover and set aside to rise until doubled in size, about 30 minutes.
3. Roll out into a rectangle about 15 × 20 inches.
4. Spread the 5 tablespoons butter across the dough. Sprinkle sugar and cinnamon over the butter. Add more if desired.
5. Roll the rectangle up from the long end. Cut into slices ½ to 1 inch thick.
6. Place the wheels on a baking sheet. Cover and set aside to rise until they are double in size, about 30 minutes.
7. Preheat oven to 500° F. Brush with beaten egg. Bake for about 10 minutes. Let cool before serving.

MAKES 20 TO 30 CINNAMON WHEELS.

Veiled Farm Girls

tilslørte bondepiker

I've been told that the name of this dessert comes from the fact that its natural ingredients are so dressed up they are unrecognizable. It is especially delicious with freshly picked apples. For this dish we picked the last apples of the season off my onkel Bjørn's trees in Oslo. You may substitute 1 to 1½ cups applesauce or puree for steps 1 and 2.

4 or 5 stewed cooking apples
¼ cup plus 2 or 3 tablespoons sugar
2 or 3 tablespoons butter
1 to 1½ cups breadcrumbs
1½ cups whipping cream
roasted almonds (optional)

1. Peel, core, and chop the apples into small pieces.
2. Cook with ¼ cup sugar and ¼ cup water until just soft. Cool.
3. Melt the butter in a frying pan over low to medium heat. Add crumbs and 2 or 3 tablespoons sugar. Fry until golden brown.
4. Whip the cream.
5. Layer the crumbs, apples or applesauce, and whipped cream in a glass dish. The final layer should be whipped cream. Garnish with a sprinkle of breadcrumbs or roasted almonds.

MAKES 8 TO 10 SERVINGS.

Norwegians brew wonderful coffee. Some housewives swear that the secret is to mix 2 eggs—with shells—with a pint of freshly ground coffee, moistening with water. They add the coffee mixture to a gallon of boiling water and cook it for several minutes before draining and serving. Hhhmmm. Skeptical, I tried it. Not bad!

Following is another old favorite from Nina of Moss.

⅋⅋

Whipped Egg Cream

kremfløte piskes

8 to 10 egg yolks (substitute: pasteurized liquid eggs)
sugar to taste
1 cup whipping cream
Nescafe coffee to taste

1. Whip egg yolks with sugar. Mix with cream.
2. Add coffee.
3. Mix well. Put in freezer until ready to serve.

MAKES 6 TO 8 SERVINGS.

*—I saw the colors
immediately change
—it quivered in
the air—it thrilled
in the yellow-white
façade—the color
dances in the stream of people
—in the brightened
and white
parasols—yellow
light blue spring costumes
—against the deep blue winter wraps . . .
I saw differently
under the influence
of the music.
The music doled out the colors.*

—Excerpted from *Open City*,
translated from Edvard Munch's diary
by Gill Holland

Edvard Munch, undoubtedly Norway's most famous artist, was born in 1863 and grew up in Norway's capital Kristiania, now called Oslo. Much of his art reflects a troubled childhood of illness, death, and grief. His mother died of tuberculosis when he was five, and his older sister Sophie died at the age of 15. A younger sister was diagnosed with mental illness at an early age. Of the five siblings only one, Andreas, ever married, only to die a few months after the wedding. Edvard himself was also often ill.

And I love life—life even sick—

Munch fell in love with art after a year at Technical School. He was instructed by Christian Krohg, Norway's leading artist of the time, who soon discovered his talent. In 1885 during a study tour in Paris, he began *The Sick Child,* a breakthrough piece based on his sister Sophie. Other works during that time were *Inger on the Beach,* painted in Åsgårdstrand, a small coastal town near Horten, and a portrait of his friend Hans Jæger. Munch's association with Jæger and his circle of radical anarchists became a crucial turning point and a source of inner unrest and conflict in Munch's life. He longed to present the truth in art.

In the autumn of 1889 another trip to Paris exposed Munch to Post-Impressionism. He found it liberating. "The camera cannot compete with a brush and canvas," he wrote, "as long as it can't be used in heaven and hell." At this time Munch did the first sketches of *The Scream*; the impressions of the soul, and not the eye, became his focus.

Three years later, Munch showed his art at the Artist's Association of Berlin. This "insult to art," as one critic described it, was closed in protest, but Munch had finally made a name for himself. He stayed in Berlin and became friends with such literati, artists, and intellectuals as the Norwegian sculptor Gustav Vigeland, the Danish writer Holger Drachmann, the Polish writer Stanislaw Przybyszewski, and the German art historian Julius Meier-Graefe.

Over the next decade Munch worked on such paintings as *Frieze of Life* and a series of landscape paintings from the Kristiania fjord, later regarded as highlights in Nordic symbolism. The evocative *Girls on the Bridge,* for example, a classic, was painted in Åsgårdstrand in the summer of 1901. By now he was firmly established in his career—and had a reputation for being one of the handsomest men in Scandinavia. Although kind-hearted and sensitive, he was also regarded as emotionally unstable, and alcohol began to cause him problems. He was plagued by the memories of a tragic love affair which had come to a dramatic end with a revolver in Åsgård-strand in the autumn of 1902 and left him with a permanently injured finger. His lover is depicted in *Death of Marat.* Munch spent eight months at a clinic in Copenhagen. While there, he was proclaimed one of Norway's greatest artists and the country awarded him the Order of St. Olav.

Munch lived in Norway for the rest of his life. For two years he stayed in Kragerø, a coastal town where he painted several classic winter landscapes, including *Winter in Kragerø,* before settling finally in Ekely in 1916 on the 12.5-acre property. Here he lived surrounded only by his pictures. Some even hung from his garden fruit trees so that their colors would weather to his liking. Although his villa is no longer standing, his winter atelier reopened in May 2000 and hosted an exhibition of his paintings.

Munch willed hundreds of paintings to the City of Oslo, and today's Munch Museum there is a must-see. Among the works are *Despair, Anxiety, Red Virginia Creeper,* a house being devoured by plants, and several of the 50 versions of *The Scream.* The National Gallery in downtown Oslo also has an exquisite Munch collection.

✺

*I*n Kragerø Edvard Munch found the inspiration for the murals he painted at the Oslo University Aula. A local sailor was the model for the old blind man in *History.*

One of the busiest resorts on the coast, Kragerø has long attracted artists and writers and scores of summer cottages dot the rocky islets offshore. The famous artist Theodor Kittelsen, a native of Kragerø, was also a regular visitor. Kittelsen's drawings of trolls are surely the best in the world!

Whenever I holiday here at a family *hytte,* my family persuades me to take the plunge into the icy fjord. It's nothing if not *deilig* (delightful)! They enjoy the water so much that they often take their bath in the fjord. I remember many summer days here chewing on long stalks on rhubarb dipped in sugar, a favorite summer snack or dessert after a dip in the water. Rhubarb is also delicious when prepared in the following way.

✺

Rhubarb Compote

1½ pounds rhubarb
1 cup sugar
1 teaspoon vanilla
3 tablespoons cornstarch
1 cup whipping cream

1. Wash rhubarb. Trim and cut into half-inch slices.
2. Combine with 1½ cups water and ¾ cup sugar and simmer until soft. Stir in vanilla.
3. Blend cornstarch with a little cold water to make a smooth, stiff paste.
4. Stirring constantly, add the cornstarch to rhubarb and cook for 5 minutes or until thick.
5. Pour into glass serving dishes. Chill in refrigerator until serving.
6. Whip cream until frothy.
7. Add ¼ cup sugar and whip until stiff.

Serve rhubarb with whipped cream or custard.

MAKES 6 TO 8 SERVINGS.

Onkel Bjørn fishing in Kragerø.

ॐ
Rhubarb Soup

rabarbra

Rhubarb soup is usually made in May, when the first shoots of rhubarb appear after winter. Anne Greta, the chef at the Borsen Spiseri in Svolvær, served us rhubarb soup on my last visit to Lofoten.

1 pound rhubarb
1 stick of cinnamon (optional)
about ⅔ cup sugar
about 4 tablespoons potato flour or cornstarch

1. Wash the rhubarb. Cut into pieces.
2. Bring 4⅓ cups water to a boil. Place the rhubarb and the cinnamon in the water.
3. Remove the cinnamon when the rhubarb is cooked, about 5 minutes.
4. Add sugar to taste. Dissolve the flour in a small amount of water. Add to mixture.

Serve hot or cold. Garnish with a mint leaf. Anne Greta serves it with a spoonful of whipping cream or vanilla ice cream.

MAKES 4 SERVINGS.

Svolvær, with a population of 4000, is the center of administration for the Lofoten Islands and the municipal center for the borough of Vågan. The town's first shop, located on Svinøya, combined fish buying with a bakery and a telegraph station. Today Svinøya is still a fishing center; as many as 200 fishermen deliver their catch here to be salted or dried. It is also a restaurant with traditional dishes from Lofoten. The adjacent Krambua, or general store, offers the same supplies as it has for the last 100 years.

In the old days Vågan hosted an annual Vågan fair when the fishermen returned to take the dried cod down from the fish racks and sell it.

❧
Apple Cake
eplekake

*T*ante Bjørg, my grandmother's sister, is famous for her *eplekake*, which is lovingly baked from the delicious apples that grow in the fruit districts along the Hardanger Fjord.

2 cups *kavring* (see following recipe or substitute melba toast crumbs)
¼ cup sugar
⅓ cup butter, melted
2½ cups applesauce
4 tablespoons (½ stick) butter
¼ cup confectioners' sugar

Preheat oven to 350° F.

1. Put crumbs and sugar in a bowl.
2. Add melted butter, tossing lightly to coat crumbs evenly.
3. Put ⅓ of the buttered crumbs in a small buttered baking dish pressing them down firmly on the bottom and sides of dish.
4. Spoon half the applesauce over the crumbs and dot with the butter. Sprinkle with half the remaining crumbs. Repeat layer of applesauce, butter, and crumbs, finishing with the crumbs.
5. Bake for about 30 minutes. Chill for several hours.

To serve, sift confectioners' sugar through decorative paper doily placed over top of cake. Lift off carefully, leaving a pattern on cake.

MAKES 6 TO 8 SERVINGS.

❧

Kavring

⅔ cup butter
¼ cup vegetable shortening
1½ cups sugar
2 eggs
1 teaspoon ground cardamom
1 cup sour cream
1 teaspoon baking soda
3½ cups all-purpose flour

1. Mix all ingredients. Refrigerate overnight.
2. Preheat oven to 350° F. Separate into 3 long rolls.
3. Bake until delicately brown. Set aside to cool. Turn oven to 375° F.
4. Slice into pieces ½-inch thick. Toast in hot oven. Brown on both sides, turning if necessary.

Keeps well in a covered container.

ℜ
Baked Apple

1 apple
½ tablespoon sugar
¼ teaspoon cinnamon
whipped cream or ice cream

Preheat oven to 425° F.

1. Remove the core from the apple, leaving the apple whole. Place a small amount of water in an ovenproof dish. Place apple in dish.
2. Mix the sugar and cinnamon together. Place mixture in the hole of the apple. Sprinkle any remaining sugar and cinnamon on the apple.
3. Bake until soft, about 20 minutes, or microwave for 3 or 4 minutes.

Serve with whipped cream or ice cream.

MAKES 1 SERVING.

✺
Marzipan

*M*arzipan is practically a staple in the diet of every good Norwegian. It can be enjoyed on its own or as a dessert ingredient. A sheet of marzipan is also often used as the final layer on *bløtkake*. Mormor sends us a marzipan pig every year for Christmas. We eat it bit by bit over the holiday.

1 cup almonds
1 cup confectioners' sugar
a little water or an egg white
dates or halved walnuts (optional)

1. Grind almonds once or twice in a food processor.
2. Add sugar and mix well with a little water or an egg white until marzipan paste forms. Make into small balls. Press down slightly with a fork. Garnish with a date or half a walnut if desired. Store tightly covered in the refrigerator.

MAKES 8 TO 12 SERVINGS.

Anthem

Reprinted with permission from the Embassy of Norway

Yes, we love with fond devotion
(The Norwegian national anthem)

Norsk Musikforlag A/S, Oslo.
Reprinted with the permission of the publisher.

Yes, we love with fond devotion
Norway's mountain domes,
rising stormlashed o'er the ocean
with their thousand homes;
Love our country while w're bending
thoughts to fathers grand,
and to saga night that's sending
dreams upon our land.

*B*jørnsterne Bjørnson wrote the words of the national anthem in the resort town of Lillehammer (literally "little hammer"), host of the 1994 Winter Olympics.

"I acknowledge no grammar-Norwegian," he once said. "I use breast-Norwegian! It should flow straight out of the breast that feels poetically, the breast that through love is able to catch it in the people and in the saga and manages to let it out again through cultured aesthetic feeling." (*Milestones of Norwegian Literature*)

Poet, playwright, author, winner of the Nobel Prize for Literature in 1903, Bjørnson loved his country and celebrated its Independence Day with particular gusto. He encouraged children to pay him a visit each year on May 17. Their parades inspired the parades of Norway's national celebrations today. His kitchen at Aulestad houses the copper pot in which he made hot chocolate for these small visitors.

"I turn my face toward Norway," were the last words Bjørnson uttered when he died in Paris in 1910. His wife returned to Norway and lived on at Aulestad. She wore white until the end of her days and was known as the White Queen.

*B*jørnson lived near Lillehammer, in a pine-clad valley at the end of a beautiful lake, which we crossed in the early morning, arriving at Aulestad—Bjørnson's home—in one of those tiny buggies called carrioles before breakfast-time. Aulestad was a big verandahed house on the side of a wooded slope, and as we climbed up to it, there was our host, with his leonine head and great shaggy white hair, awaiting us, his arms stretched out in welcome, like a patriarch—though as a matter of fact he was little beyond sixty. He was an impressive figure of a man, with his broad sturdy shoulders, his eyes and nose like an eagle's—half lion, half eagle, so to say—suggesting immense strength and magnetic force. He seemed indeed like a hero from the old Scandinavian sagas come to life again, and, as he embraced us, we felt swept up into a larger, keener air. We noticed that he carried a bath towel over his shoulder, which he immediately explained.

"I am off for my bath in the woods," he said, "will you join me?" He spoke English, I may say, like an Englishman.

It was an heroic welcome, but we were game, and presently the three of us were tramping through the woods till we came to where a mountain stream fell in a torrent of white water down the face of a rock. Planks had been placed at the foot of the fall. "This is my shower bath," said Bjørnson, as he stripped, and there presently he stood, firm as a rock, beneath the cataract, the water pouring over his strong shoulders, his white head white as the foam, and shouting with joy of the morning. So might some great old water-god have stood and laughed amid the sun-flashing spray. It was a picture of elemental energy never to be forgotten, and, as one watched him there, one could well understand the power that made him the uncrowned king of his country.

Then, nothing loath, we repaired to the house for breakfast, and here again all was "saga," and one seemed to be seated in the hall of Sigurd the Volsung; for the master of the house and his lady, beautiful and commanding like her lord, sat at the end of a long table, royally side by side, on a slightly raised dais, with my friend and me, their guests, to right and left of them. One expected an aged harper to appear at any moment. Below us sat Bjørnson's daughter, Bergliot, named after his greatest poem, a glorious girl made out of gold and the blue sky, with whom, married men though we were, Johnson and I at once fell hopelessly in love. The tall brothers of the old ballads were not lacking, and other members of the household lined the table. The breakfast, too, belonged to "saga"—no shredded wheat and glass-of-milk business, but the robust Norwegian breakfast of heroes, roast meats, and pungently spiced and smoked fishes, and, if not exactly horns of mead, bumpers of salt and aperitifs of schnapps.

—Excerpted from *The Romantic 90s*,
by Richard Le Gallienne

$\mathcal{M}$olde was once the childhood home of Bjørnson. Like many of the towns that sheltered King Håkon on his flight from Oslo, Molde was nearly destroyed during the German invasion of World War II. Today a small monument on the slopes shows where King Håkon and Crown Prince Olav stood, helpless, while Molde was bombed to the ground.

When it became possible to reach the town, it was discovered that the Molde rose, a luxuriant flower unique to the town, had been completely destroyed. Although the town of Molde was rebuilt, its rose was sorely missed. A few years ago, a visiting German horticulturalist heard this story. Upon his return to Germany, he set about creating a rose like the Molde Rose. His creation was recently presented to Molde.

✿

Almond Cake

mandelbunn

3 eggs
1⅓ cups sugar or confectioners' sugar
¼ teaspoon baking powder
1⅓ cups ground almonds

1. Beat the eggs. Add sugar slowly while tasting. You might decide to use less sugar.
2. Blend the egg and sugar mixture with baking powder and almonds. (You can substitute slivered almonds for ground almonds. The cake will be slightly heavier, but still delicious.) Place dough in a round spring pan.
3. Do not preheat the oven. Bake at 350° F for about 50 minutes.

Serve with whipped cream or ice cream.

MAKES 10 TO 12 SERVINGS.

ﷺ
Grandmother's Yo Yo Cake

Mormor's Yo Yo kake

*A*gain, stores like Haram-Christensen Corp. listed at the end of the book, carry specialty items like the vanilla sugar called for below. As a substitute, simply add a few drops of vanilla to sugar.

¾ cup sugar
1 egg
2 tablespoon warm water
⅞ cup all-purpose flour
1 teaspoon baking powder

ICING

⅝ cup butter, melted
2 teaspoons vanilla sugar
food coloring

1. Mix sugar, egg, and the warm water well. Add flour with baking powder. Knead. Place in refrigerator for 1 hour.
2. Preheat oven to 350° F. Roll into sausages about 4 cm in diameter. Cut in very thin pieces, about ½-cm thick. My grandmother uses an egg cup to make the top and bottom cakes even.
3. Bake on greased cookie sheet until light yellow, about 20 minutes. Set aside to cool.
4. Make the icing by mixing the butter and vanilla sugar. Color the icing with food coloring to make the cakes decorative. When the cakes are cold, place them in pairs, one on top of the other with a thin layer of icing in between.

MAKES ABOUT 7 TO 10 DOUBLE-DECKER CAKES.

❧
Chocolate Roll

sjokolade rull

3 eggs
⅔ cup granulated sugar
5 tablespoons potato flour (or cornstarch)
2 teaspoons cocoa
2 teaspoons baking powder

FILLING

⅔ cup confectioners' sugar
1½ stick butter
1 teaspoon vanilla

Preheat oven to 375° F.

1. Beat the eggs and granulated sugar together. Add the flour, cocoa, and baking powder.
2. Roll dough into a rectangle shape. Place on well-buttered wax paper on a cookie sheet.
3. Bake for 10 minutes in hot oven.
4. Coat another piece of wax paper with sugar. Remove dough from paper and place dough on sugar-coated wax paper. Set aside to cool.
5. Make the filling by mixing the confectioners' sugar, butter, and vanilla. Spread the filling evenly over the dough. Roll into a long roll. Wrap in the sugar-coated paper and refrigerate overnight.

MAKES 12 TO 16 SERVINGS.

Holiday and Party Foods

Kjære Gud, jeg har det godt
Takk for alt som jeg har fått
Du er snild som holder av meg
Kjære Gud gå aldri fra meg.

Dear God, all is well.
Thank you for everything I have.
You are kind who watches over me
Dear God, never leave me.

ℜ*ransekake* serves as a beautiful centerpiece for holiday parties, weddings, and confirmations. It is a must for any special event—but it's not easy to make. Although the best—and easiest—way to bake the dough is in *kransekake* molds (see Contacts, page 279), a series of graduated ring-shaped pans, you can also simply draw the rings on pieces of ovenproof paper and pipe the dough right onto the paper. The rings will be stacked on top of each other to form a tower, so it is important that they are graduated in size. The smallest should be 5 or 6 inches in diameter; each additional ring should be about an inch larger.

ஜ

Kransekake

𝓨ou'll find that *kransekake* tastes best if you use a combination of blanched and unblanched almonds. Blanch almonds by pouring boiling water over them and then steaming them until the hulls are easy to remove. If you use only blanched almonds, your cake will be an attractive light color but will probably be less flavorful.

You can also use ready-made marzipan available in specialty stores (see list on page 279).

5½ cups almonds
5½ cups confectioners' sugar
4 egg whites, lightly beaten
2 tablespoon flour (optional)

ICING

1 cup confectioners' sugar
1 egg white

1. Wash and thoroughly dry almonds. (You can be sure they are dry by letting them stand, covered, for 24 hours.)
2. Grind the almonds twice, adding the confectioners' sugar the second time.
3. Add the egg whites slowly, mixing well. Do not allow the mixture to become too moist. If it seems too moist, add a little flour and confectioners' sugar. (If the cake is not moist enough, add a little egg white.) You may want to bake a small sample first to make sure that the dough is the proper consistency. Over a low heat, knead the dough until it is almost too hot to handle.
4. Cover the dough and set aside for 10 minutes. Preheat oven to 400° F.
5. Grease ring-shaped *kransekake* pans with unsalted butter or cooking oil. Roll out small portions to fit the pans, each ½ inch thick. Cut any uneven edges with a knife so that you'll have a balanced cake. If you don't have *kransekake* pans, follow directions above and form rings from dough that has been cut into the appropriate sizes. Place rings on a well-greased cookie sheet.
6. Bake cookie sheet in the middle of the oven until the rings are brown. They should be firm on the outside and chewy inside. This takes 12 to 15 minutes. Do not overbake.
7. Set aside in a cool place to cool quickly. When almost cool, carefully remove from pans.
8. To make icing, stir confectioners' sugar and egg white together until the icing is thick enough to be used as a glue to stick the layers together. Glue the rings together with icing in ascending order. When the rings are stacked on top of each other, any remaining icing works well as an extra adhesive. Decorate with zigzags of icing and small Norwegian flags and candies. Attach the decorations with caramel.

MAKES A 16-RING CAKE, ABOUT 15 SERVINGS.

❧

Easy Kransekake *II*

3 cans or 1½ pounds almond paste
3 egg whites
1½ cup granulated sugar

ICING

1 egg white
3 or 4 drops of vinegar
1 cup confectioners' sugar

Preheat oven to 325° F.

1. Mix almond paste, egg whites, and sugar together with a mixer. Roll out like dough.
2. Grease a flat surface. Form rings on the surface. (Follow steps 5 through 7 in the preceding recipe for *kransekake.*)
3. Mix the egg whites, vinegar, and sugar together for icing. Follow step 8 in the preceding recipe for *kransekake.*

❦
Fyrstekake

*A*ccording to my mormor, who makes the best *fyrstekake* in Norway, the secret to a delicious cake is the more butter the better!

1 cup all-purpose flour
1 teaspoon baking powder
⅔ cup butter
2 eggs, separated
½ cup granulated sugar
⅔ cup to 1 cup finely chopped almonds or hazelnuts
1¼ cups granulated or confectioners' sugar

Preheat oven to 350° F.

1. Mix flour, baking powder, butter, egg yolks, and ½ cup granulated sugar together for dough. Set about ¼ of the dough aside. Spread the rest of the dough in a round 8-inch pan and a little up on the sides.
2. Mix the almonds with the egg whites and 1¼ cups granulated or confectioners' sugar. Add a small amount of lukewarm water if necessary.
3. Place almond mixture on dough.
4. Make long strips from the remaining dough. Cover the filling with crisscross stripes. Bake for 45 minutes.

Particularly good in the summer served with ice cream.

MAKES 14 TO 16 SERVINGS.

VANILLA CREAM

fyrstekake med vanilje krem

Follow directions above but replace step 2 with filling: mix 1 (3.4-ounce) package instant vanilla pudding mix and 2 cups whole milk. You may also use custard or applesauce for filling. The custard-filled cake is particularly tasty with chocolate frosting.

*A*t Easter everyone heads to the mountains. Oslo residents visit their *hytter*. In Karasjok and Kautokeino the Sami hold reindeer races and celebrate baptisms and weddings. The Islanders are busy fishing for the schools of cod for which they've waited all year.

Easter is also a time of *fastelavnsboller*, cream- and jam-filled buns sprinkled with confectioners' sugar, and *fastelavnsris*. Children celebrate *fastelavns*, the only day of the year when they are allowed to spank their parents. They tie birch branches and colorful feathers together for the spanking.

Before fasting for Lent everyone fills up on delicious *fastelavnsboller*.

❦
Fastelavnsboller

½ cup sugar
1 teaspoon cardamom
4 cups all-purpose flour
1 cup butter
4 tablespoons (4 packets) yeast
2 cups whole milk, lukewarm
beaten egg or whole milk

FILLING

1 cup heavy cream
2 tablespoons chopped almonds
2 tablespoons sugar
3 egg yolks
pinch of salt

1. Mix sugar, cardamom, and flour. Crumble butter into mixture.
2. Add yeast to lukewarm milk a little at a time. Add to flour mixture. Knead dough well for 15 minutes. Cover and set aside to rise for 30 minutes.

3. Knead dough again. Separate into about 20 round balls. Cover and set aside to rise again for 30 minutes.

4. Preheat oven to 350° F. Brush each ball with a beaten egg or milk. Bake for 20 to 30 minutes. Remove from oven and turn off oven.

5. Whip cream, almonds, sugar, egg yolks, and salt together until thick.

6. Cut the rolls in half and place 1 tablespoon of filling in the center of each roll. Return to the still-warm oven for 10 minutes.

MAKES ABOUT 20 *BOLLER.*

❧

> "*W*e have learned this, too, that there is something greater than our personal affairs and wishes: our country, our people, this Norway which has been sustained through adversity, ravaged, pillaged, and poor; but free—and our own in a deeper, more intimate sense than ever before."
>
> —Quotation from Sigrid Undset in
> *A History of Norway*, Karen Larsen

*N*orwegians celebrate their Independence Day, or *Syttende Mai* (17th of May), with gusto. The streets are full of music and parades, and people dance and sing in their traditional *bunad* (folk costume). Poet Henrik Wergeland and author Bjørnstjerne Bjørnson jointly proclaimed *Syttende Mai* a day for children, who still process in parades with bands playing national songs. The children of Oslo march past *Slottet*, the royal palace, to salute the king, who waves from the balcony with his family as they pass.

Norway first declared its independence and wrote a constitution on May 17, 1814. Although the country was forced to accept Swedish rule later that year, the Norwegian Constitution remained in effect until 1905, when Norway truly became independent.

For many centuries before its independence the land had seen much inner conflict. Following a long decline after the Viking period, Norway was united with Sweden in 1319 and with Denmark in 1380. In 1397 Danish Queen Margaret made the triple union of Norway, Sweden, and Denmark official. Copenhagen was the undisputed capital of the kingdom. Sweden dropped out in 1521, but Norway and Denmark remained united until 1814.

It was Danish king Christian IV who first took a real interest in the country, even giving Oslo the compliment of renaming it Christiania in 1624. Norway, not content with the Danish government, began to consider self-rule. The separatist movements in Norway continued to grow through the Napoleanic wars. After repeated requests, the Norwegians did finally get their own bank in 1811—and came one step closer to independence.

Norway finally separated from Denmark with the Treaty of Kiel on January 14, 1814. After declaring itself independent from Denmark, a National Assembly of 112 met at Eidsvold Iron works outside Christiania to lay the foundation of a constitution.

One representative wrote: "Here was to be seen a selection of men from all parts of the realm, of all ranks and dialects, men from court circles as well as landowners come together in no set order for the sacred purpose of laying the foundations for the rebirth of the nation."

Its union with Sweden was dissolved in 1905. On November 18, 1905, the Storting unanimously elected Prince Carl of Denmark King of Norway, who immediately sent a telegram of acceptance. He took the name Håkon VII, gave his little son Alexander the name Olav, and chose as his motto "*Alt for Norge*" (Everything for Norway) from the words of Norwegian poet Wergeland of Akershus: "*O hvad fryd for dine taarne, saa du Haakons tid igjen*" (Oh, what joy for your spires to see once more the age of Håkon).

May 17 has been celebrated every year since 1905. During the German occupation of Norway from April 9, 1940, to May 7, 1945, the writer Nordahl Grieg wrote:

> *Now stands the flagpole bare*
> *Behind Eidsvoll's budding trees,*
> *But in such an hour as this,*
> *We know what freedom is.*

May 17 also celebrates the arrival of spring. Traditionally Norwegians serve *koldt bord* with *spekemat* including smoked salmon with omelet and, of course, scrambled eggs (below). Traditional cream cakes like *kransekake* and *fyrstekaker* are also a part of the celebration.

May 17th celebration. Look closely and you can see the king waving from the palace balcony.

OLSOK

Norway's pagan traditions comfortably co-exist with its very strong Christian roots. Christianity arrived about a thousand years ago with the Christian princess Sunniva, who fled Ireland by boat to escape betrothal to a heathen chieftain. According to legend, she landed on the island of Selja, near today's Kristiansund, where she was forced to hide from the Viking heathens and their leader Håkon Jarl. She prayed to God to break down the mountain and bury them, and miraculously an avalanche tumbled down. Her soul soared to heaven in a spire of light.

Viking chieftain Olav Tryggvason (also known as "Crow Bone" for his ability to predict the future from bird bones) heard about Sunniva's great escape while fighting battles in a foreign land. In 996 he exhumed her bones and found her corpse unmarked. Awestruck, he determined to convert the Norwegian population to Christianity. The following year, Gulating, the Viking court and parliament, formally accepted Christianity. Sunniva's body was placed in a casket and taken to the diocese in Bergen, and Selja became the site of the Selja Kloster monastery, the ruins of which still stand.

It was Viking Olav Haraldsson who indirectly established the Church. A strong Christian, Haraldsson attempted to convert the people, but found the old gods hard to banish. After a heroic death in battle on July 29, 1030, at Stiklestad, however, miracles occurred at his gravesite by the River Nid. He was declared Olav the Holy the patron saint of Norway, and people began to convert. Pilgrims still visit his burial site for its healing powers. The festival of Olsok, the most important celebration of the church, commemorates the death of St. Olav. It is said that the weather on the day of Olsok augurs the forecast for fall. If Olsok falls on a wet day, fall will be rainy. A clear Olsok predicts a dry and sunny fall, and if Olsok is cold the farmers must watch that their grain doesn't freeze. *Rømmegrøt* (see recipe following) is perhaps the most popular dish served at Olsok, which is also harvest time. The women used to carry it to workers in the fields in special wooden containers. The rich *rømmegrøt* is made almost entirely of cream. The fat that bubbles out of it is served separately with cinnamon and sugar.

It took 200 years for Norway to be Christianized. Once converted, the Norwegians set about building churches. While other European architects constructed their cathedrals out of stone, the Norwegians used wood. After all, the outstanding craftsmanship of the Viking ships had already proved its success. In fact, many historians believe that the same craftsmen built both ships and churches, a theory based on the close resemblance of these churches and Viking ships to each other.

The first generation of Norwegian churches only stood for about 100 years before their posts rotted. In the next century the need for more solid constructions became obvious. By resting the planks or "staves" upon sills, architects introduced a way to raise the walls above ground level and protect them against rot. Like the previous churches, these "stave" churches were dark and windowless. It was necessary to keep both the cold and the Devil out. Many are beautifully ornate, however. The largest and most ornate is the Borgund church. Urnes Stave Church is on the UNESCO World Heritage List. The stave church of Heddal, the largest in Norway, boasts a thirteenth-century bishop's chair with a design that tells the saga of Sigurd the Dragonslayer, a pagan story told by Christians as well. They conveniently cast the Viking as Jesus and the dragon as the Devil. Twenty-nine of the churches still stand today.

With places to worship, Christianity took hold in Norway. The Reformation arrived in 1536 and brought an emphasis on personal faith. By 1739 the Church had backed the establishment of general education in Norway. Schools, which were founded to teach the people Christianity, eventually introduced classes in reading and writing as well. Today about 96% of Norwegians are estimated to be members of the Lutheran church, and confirmation is taken seriously. Candidates are even required to answer questions about their lessons before the entire congregation.

In lean years *rømmegrøt* was served only for such special occasions like Olsok or a birth. During holiday seasons, however, farmers always left the porridge out for the mythical gnomelike housespirit *nisse* to ensure his good temper. Although *nisser* often get into mischief, they do protect their farms. The tradition of the *nisse* dates from pagan times. According to legend, he is always related to the farmer who first cleared the land.

𝔈

Sour Cream Porridge

rømmegrøt

4 cups thick sour cream
1½ cups all-purpose flour
2 cups whole milk, or 1 cup sweet plus 1 cup sour milk, heated
½ teaspoon salt

1. Cover the sour cream and cook over medium heat for 8 to 10 minutes. Sprinkle about ½ cup of the flour into the cream. Mix. Let the sour cream bubble until the butter separates, about 15 minutes.
2. Over low heat, stir occasionally. Remove as much butter as desired. Set aside in a warm place.
3. Add the remaining 1 cup flour. Mix well.
4. Add hot milk slowly while stirring. Scrape the edges of the pan. Cook porridge 6 or 7 more minutes.
5. Add salt to taste.

Serve with sugar and cinnamon and the warm butter. Serve with flat-bread and dried, cured meat for a summertime favorite.

MAKES ABOUT 8 SERVINGS.

*R*ømmegrøt *is often part of the Norwegian wedding feast. In Norway weddings are elaborate affairs. Every region has its own traditions. The beautiful little medieval church in Ullensvang, for example, often hosts the traditional Hardanger crown weddings, which have recently come back into fashion. In the old days of crown weddings the bride rode to church on horseback escorted by fiddlers playing Hardanger fiddles (pictured above). She wore an ornate, heavily decorated gold or silver wedding crown, which was often an old family heirloom. (Although most were melted down during the years of Danish rule to pay the silver tax imposed by the government, several original crowns are on display in museums around the country.) The bride also brought her beautifully decorated wedding chest full of linens, new clothes, silverware, and other possessions for her new home. Her single name and the year of the wedding were printed on the side of the chest. Tidemand and Gude's* The Bridal Journey in Hardanger *shows such a wedding at the Ullensvang church.*

 The Hardanger fiddle dates to 1651. Many instruments were destroyed in the late 1800s because the music produced by them was considered "devilish." You can learn to play the fiddle at the Rauland Academy in Telemark.

Hearts of Christians all should glow
With the warmth of Christmas fare,
Honey-sweet,
Heaped for all the world to eat,
Should it chance to enter there,
Decked with sprigs of roses gay,
As for festal holiday.
Woe! Woe!

—Henrik Wergeland from
Milestones of Norwegian Literature

Christmas in Norway is like no other. A jolly, red-suited *julenisse* (Christmas elf) visits every house on Christmas Eve to deliver presents to the children. Farmers leave *rømmegrøt* (cream porridge) for the *fjøsnisse* (cow-barn pixie) to ensure that he'll protect their farm. Food is left on the Christmas table for the dead, who are said to travel about in great numbers during this season. *Julenek*, a sheaf of corn and oats saved from the summer harvest, decorates lampposts for the winter birds to enjoy on Christmas Eve. All the farm animals get special tidbits—even the cows munch on salted herring. Skiers follow the cross-country paths lit by the glow of torches.

The quantity of the food served at Christmas is said to augur poverty or plenty in the year to come, and preparations for Christmas go on for weeks. *Juleøl* (Christmas beer) is brewed, numerous pork dishes are prepared, Christmas cookies are baked, and the smell of *julekake* fills the countryside. *Juleøl* can be traced to the time when people drank from beer horns during Joulu, festivities for the Norse gods Odin and Freya (who gave us the names of Wednesday and Friday), and Njord (god of prosperity, father of Freya). The beer survived Christianity simply because no one would give it up.

The main event during the holiday season is Christmas Eve. After dinner, families join hands and circle the Christmas tree singing carols. Finally everyone opens presents.

Every region of Norway features a slightly different holiday menu. Along the coast the main dish is fresh cod, halibut, or *lutefisk* (see page 96). In eastern Norway traditional Christmas fare is pork ribs with pork sausage patties (see page 131) and Christmas sausages. This tradition dates to Joulu, when a pig was sacrificed to the goddess Freya. Pigs made from marzipan (*marsipangris*) also figure prominently. The people of Trøndelag feast on both *lutefisk* and roast pork. In the west you'll be served lamb, dried and salted as it was in the Viking days and served hot and steaming on a bed of birch twigs (see page 129). Other Christmas specialties include sweet and salted delicacies like head cheese (see page 263), smoked leg of lamb, marinated herrings (see page 15), and the standard pork sausages and meatballs enjoyed year-round. A traditional meal in Røros is lightly salted trout and sour cream porridge (see page 256) served on the same plate.

The following rice porridge, often served for Saturday suppers (*grøtmiddag*) before a late *aftens* and regularly on Fridays at nursing homes in Oslo, is delicious—and extra special on Christmas Eve. Housewives place a single almond in the porridge, and whoever gets the almond in their bowl wins a prize. I won the almond one Christmas in Norway, and it was quite thrilling. The prize is usually a marzipan pig.

January 6, the Day of the Three Kings who followed the star to find Jesus, marks the end of Christmas. Celebrations officially end on January 13, the twentieth day after Christmas.

❧
Creamed Rice

risengrynsgrøt

*T*his very filling porridge is usually served alone or with butter, sugar, and cinnamon.

½ cup long-grain rice
2 cups whole milk
¼ teaspoon salt

1. Rinse the rice 3 times in water. Bring 1 cup water to a boil.
2. Add the rice slowly while stirring. Cover and simmer until most of the water has been absorbed by the rice.
3. Add boiling milk. Cover and let simmer for up to 2 hours or until it reaches desired consistency of porridge. Stir occasionally.

Add salt before serving. Serve with butter, sugar, and cinnamon. In summer serve with *spekemat.*

MAKES ABOUT 3 SERVINGS.

❧
Christmas Pork Ribs

ribbe

2 or 3 pounds pork ribs
salt and pepper

1. Saw through the bone so the ribs can be pulled apart for serving.
2. Rub with salt and pepper. Cover and set aside for a day or two in the refrigerator.
3. Preheat oven to 425° F. Place roast in a roasting dish.
4. Pour 1 cup water into the roasting dish. Cover the ribs with foil.
5. Roast in the middle of the oven for 30 to 40 minutes.
6. Remove the foil and lower the oven temperature to 400°F. Roast spare ribs an additional 1½ hours and midribs 2 to 2½ hours.
7. Let stand for 20 minutes before carving.

Serve with pork sausage patties, Christmas sausages, *surkål* (see page 149), lingonberries, and any other family favorites.

MAKES 4 SERVINGS.

⅋

Nina's Ribbe

2 pounds boneless fresh ham with pork rind
1½ teaspoons salt
dash of pepper
2 cups water or stock
all-purpose flour

Preheat oven to 350° F.

1. Rub the meat well with salt and pepper. Place in a roasting pan.
2. Bake about 20 minutes per pound or until your meat thermometer reads 135° F to 144° F. Set aside to rest for 10 or 15 minutes.
3. Mix the meat drippings with boiling water or stock until you have about 2 cups liquid. Pour into bowl.
4. Mix a small amount of flour and water together. Mix well with drippings. Let simmer for 5 or 10 minutes.
5. Remove the crisp rind from the meat.

   Serve with boiled potatoes, *surkål*, and prunes.

MAKES 4 OR 5 SERVINGS.

Sweet and salted delicacies also make up the Christmas feast. Following is a simple recipe for traditional headcheese, a good sandwich meat. Headcheese is also available ready-made in most parts of Norway.

❧

Head Cheese
sylte

5 pounds pork shoulder, cut in 3 or 4 pieces
2½ pounds veal shoulder, cut in 3 or 4 pieces
2 teaspoons salt
pepper, cinnamon, allspice, cloves

1. Place pork and veal in a deep pan. Cover with hot water.
2. Add salt. Cook for about 2 hours or until the meat falls off the bones. (Cooking time depends on the size of the meat pieces.)
3. Line a pan or bowl with a hot cloth. Cut meat into small pieces. Place a layer of the meat pieces in the bottom of the pan. Press down well with a fork. Sprinkle with pepper, cinnamon, allspice, and ground cloves. Add more salt if desired.
4. Continue to layer meat and spices until pan is filled almost to the top or until all the meat is gone. Cover with a cloth. Place a weight on top of the cloth. (A board or plate with a brick or iron on top works well.) Refrigerate several hours before slicing.

MAKES ABOUT 12 SERVINGS.

Dovregubben, the king of the trolls, lives in the Dovre mountains, where the following story takes place.

THE CAT OF DOVRE

There was once a man up in Finnmark who caught a big white bear and he set out to take it to the King of Denmark. And it so happened that he came to the mountains of Dovre on Christmas Eve, and he went into a cottage where there lived a man by the name of Halvor. Here he asked for a night's shelter for himself and his white bear.

"Heaven help us all!" said the cottager. "We can give no shelter to strangers tonight, for every Christmas Eve there come so many trolls here that we all have to move out of the house and we have no roof over our own heads."

"Oh, I think you can still put me up," said the man. "My bear can sleep under the stove here, and the closet will do for me."

In the end, he was allowed to stay. Then the family moved out, having prepared a table laden with cream porridge and lye fish and sausages and all the good things that belong to a festive board.

All of a sudden, the trolls came in. Some were big and some were small, some had long tails and some had no tails, and some had long, long noses. And they ate and they drank and they tasted all the dishes.

But one of the little trolls caught sight of the white bear asleep under the stove. And he seized a piece of sausage, roasted it hot on the end of a fork, and toddled along and thrust it under the nose of the white bear, crying, "Pussy want a sausage?"

And then the white bear started up with a mighty growl and chased the whole pack of them helter-skelter out of the house.

One year later, Halvor was in the forest on the afternoon of Christmas Eve cutting wood for the Christmas season, for he was expecting the trolls again. While he was busily chopping, he heard a voice call from the forest, "Halvor! Halvor!"

"Yes," said Halvor.

"Have you still got that big cat of yours?"

"Yes, she's at home asleep under the stove," said Halvor. "And now she has a litter of seven kittens who are all much bigger and angrier than she is!"

"Well, we won't be coming to visit you any more!" shouted the troll from the depths of the forest. And since that time the trolls have never eaten Christmas dinner at Halvor's cottage in Dovre.

—Excerpted from *A Time for Trolls, Fairy Tales from Norway*

*H*ouseholds across Norway serve the traditional cookies of Christmas. They are called *inne og ute kaker* (in-and-out-of-the-box cookies) because a hostess must bring them out every time a guest arrives at her house and then put them away again.

The following are recipes for the most traditional Christmas cookies.

❧
Gingersnaps

¾ cup corn syrup
¾ cup sugar
¾ cup cream
½ cup butter
2 cups all-purpose flour
¼ teaspoon pepper
¼ teaspoon ginger
¼ teaspoon aniseed
¼ teaspoon cinnamon
¾ teaspoon salt
¾ teaspoon baking soda
blanched almonds
egg white (optional)

1. Bring the syrup, sugar, and cream to a boil.
2. Add the butter and let it melt. Let cool until lukewarm.
3. Sift in the flour, pepper, ginger, aniseed, cinnamon, salt, and baking soda. Mix well. Refrigerate overnight.
4. The next day, preheat oven to 325° F. Roll the dough very thin. Cut out thin cookies and place each cookie on a greased cookie sheet. Place half a blanched almond on each cookie. Brush with egg white if desired. Bake for about 5 minutes.

MAKES ABOUT 2 DOZEN COOKIES.

❧

Poor Man's Cookies

fattigman

6 egg yolks
¼ cup sugar
1 tablespoon butter, melted
⅓ cup heavy cream, whipped
1 teaspoon ground cardamom
2 cups all-purpose flour, sifted
½ teaspoon salt
butter for frying
confectioners' sugar, sifted

1. Beat the egg yolks until thick and yellow.
2. Gradually beat in sugar.
3. Gently stir in butter.
4. Fold in whipped cream and cardamom. Sift flour and salt together. Gradually fold into yolk mixture until dough is soft.
5. Refrigerate for several hours or until chilled.
6. Divide dough in half.
7. On lightly floured surface, roll each piece until about ⅛ inch thick. Cut into 3 inch × ¾-inch strips. Cut a slit lengthwise in center of each and pull one end through.
8. Fry a few at a time in butter in a deep pot until a light golden brown, 1 or 2 minutes.
9. Remove and drain on paper towels. While warm, sprinkle confectioners' sugar over each cookie.

MAKES 5 DOZEN COOKIES.

❧

Oatmeal Cookies

havremakroner

½ cup (1 stick) margarine
½ cup sugar
1 egg
½ cup all-purpose flour
½ cup oatmeal

Preheat oven to 350° F.

1. Melt the margarine. Stir in sugar, egg, and flour.
2. Add the oatmeal. Separate into golf ball-size portions. Bake on greased cookie sheet for 20 to 30 minutes or until light brown.

MAKES 12 COOKIES.

✌

Mother Monsen

Mor Monsen

5 eggs
1⅛ cups sugar
1⅛ cups butter, slightly melted
1⅛ cups all-purpose flour
coarse sugar (optional)
slivered almonds or Champagne raisins (currants)

Preheat oven to 350° F.

1. Add eggs to sugar one at a time, mixing thoroughly. Whip mixture well.
2. Mix butter and flour.
3. Stir both mixtures together. Sprinkle coarse sugar and almonds or raisins if desired over dough.
4. Bake on wax paper in a 9 × 12-inch pan until golden brown, 30 to 45 minutes.

Garnish with slivered almonds or currants.

MAKES 20 TO 30 COOKIES.

❧
Doughnuts

smultering

3 eggs
1¼ cups sugar
2½ cups sour cream
¾ cup whole milk
4 teaspoons horn salt or baking powder
2 teaspoons cardamom
3¼ cups wheat flour
butter or oil for frying

1. Beat the eggs and sugar.
2. Whisk the sour cream. Add the milk, salt, cardamom, and flour. Blend gently. Let stand overnight.
3. Roll into ½-inch-thick sheets. Cut out doughnuts and deep-fry in butter or oil.

MAKES ABOUT 3 DOZEN DOUGHNUTS.

In Norway *krumkake* is made with a krumkake iron; see picture. You might have to experiment a little your first few times making *krumkake*. The humidity in some parts of America makes these and other crisp Norwegian cakes difficult to make.

Krumkake iron.

❧
Crumb Cookies

krumkake

3 eggs
¾ cup sugar
¾ cup butter
¾ cup all-purpose flour
½ teaspoon cardamom

1. Beat the eggs and sugar until stiff.
2. Melt the butter. Let cool. Mix the butter, flour, and cardamom together.
3. Add to the beaten egg mixture. Knead. Cover and set aside to rise for about an hour.
4. Put 1 teaspoon dough on hot *krumkake* iron (medium temperature) and turn immediately. Turn occasionally until golden brown on both sides.
5. Place the golden cookies on a terry cloth towel or paper towel. Roll into desired shape. *Krumkake* usually looks like an ice cream cone and is filled with whipped cream. Other shapes include a handle or a pencil.

Store in a tin or freeze. Garnish with cloudberries or raspberries.

MAKES ABOUT 2 DOZEN COOKIES.

❧
Sand Cakes

sandkaker

*I*f you mix confectioners' sugar and granulated sugar, it might be easier to remove the cakes from the *sandkaker* tins.

1 cup butter or margarine
1 cup sugar
1 egg
1 teaspoon almond extract or ½ cup blanched almonds (optional)
3 cups sifted all-purpose flour

1. Thoroughly cream butter and sugar together.
2. Add egg. Beat well.
3. Add almond extract or grind the almonds in a food processor and add ground almonds.
4. Stir in flour.
5. Preheat oven to 325° F. Pinch of a small ball of dough and place in the center of the *sandkaker* tins. Press dough evenly and as thinly as possible over bottom and up along the edges of the tins. The tins are like individual cupcake tins but with different shapes. Bake for 10 to 15 minutes or until golden brown. Let cool before removing from tins. To remove, invert tins and tap lightly.

Serve with whipped cream, berries, and/or fruit.

MAKES 4 OR 5 DOZEN COOKIES.

❧❧

Serina Cakes

serinakaker

1¼ cup all-purpose flour
2 teaspoons baking powder
2 teaspoons vanilla sugar
¾ cup butter
1 egg, beaten
½ cup granulated sugar
1 egg, beaten (optional)
almonds, chopped (optional)

Preheat oven to 325° F.

1. Sift the flour, baking powder, and vanilla sugar together. Crumble the butter into the mixture.
2. Add the beaten egg and granulated sugar. Knead thoroughly.
3. Roll dough into the shape of a sausage, about 1 inch in diameter. Cut and shape into golf ball-size balls.
4. Place on a cookie sheet, and press down gently with a fork.
5. Brush with egg and sprinkle with chopped almonds or coarse sugar if desired.
6. Bake for about 20 minutes or until golden brown.

MAKES 30 TO 40 COOKIES.

℀
Goro

Goro is a challenge for any cook, and humidity can make it especially difficult. It is easier to make in a cold kitchen. These days many people make *goro* with an electric iron. In the old days Mormor and her sister Bjørg made it together.

1 cup whipping cream
3 egg yolks
⅔ cup sugar
6 cups all-purpose flour, sifted
1 teaspoon cardamom
3 cups butter

1. Whip the cream.
2. Beat the egg yolks and sugar together. Add the cream. Add flour. Mix well.
3. Gradually add cardamom and 2 cups butter. Knead dough well. Roll it out in a thick layer. Spread the remaining 1 cup butter thinly across the dough. Fold over and roll once more. Refrigerate overnight.
4. Roll the dough, and cut into flat pieces the size of the *goro* iron. (A waffle iron is sufficient.) Bake on ungreased iron until golden and crisp. (If necessary wipe off any fat that trickles off the iron.) Cut apart while still hot. Let cool completely before serving.

Serve with sprinkled sugar.

MAKES 12 DOZEN COOKIES.

❧
Christmas Bread
julekake

4 cups whole milk
1½ cups sugar
½ cup butter
3 teaspoons cardamom seed
4 packages (4 tablespoons) dry yeast
1 teaspoon salt
2 cups raisins
8 ounces candied citron
4 ounces lemon peel
2 eggs, beaten
about 12 cups all-purpose flour

ICING

1 egg yolk
1 teaspoon vanilla
1 tablespoon sugar

1. Heat milk and sugar. Add butter and cardamom seed.
2. When butter has melted, set aside to cool to lukewarm.
3. Add yeast to dissolve. Add salt, raisins, citron, lemon peel, and eggs. Work well together.
4. Add enough flour to make a firm and elastic dough. Cover and set aside to rise in a warm place until doubled in size, about an hour.
5. Knead well and form into two round loaves.
6. Place on greased pie pan and cover. Set aside until doubled in size, about an hour.
7. Preheat oven to 350° F. Bake for about 1 hour.
8. Mix egg yolk, vanilla, and sugar together for icing. Brush the loaves with the icing immediately when they come out of oven.

MAKES 2 LARGE OR 3 SMALL ROUND OR REGULAR LOAVES.

Contacts

Børsen Spiseri
Gunnar Bergs vei 2
PO Box 74
8300 Svolvær
tel. 47-76-06-99-30

Den norske bokbyen
6848 Fjærland
tel. 47-57-69-22-10

Den Norske Hytteformidling (NOWASOL)
PO Box 309
Sentrum, N-0103 Oslo
tel. 47-22-35-62-70 or 47-55-52-06-88

Directorate for Nature Management
7485 Trondheim
tel. 47-73-58-05-00

Embassy of Norway
2720 34th St. NW
Washington, DC
tel. 1-202-333-6000

Finnholmen Brygge
PO Box 47
8312 Henningsvær
tel. 47-76-06-99-60

Finse 1222
N-3590 Finse
tel. 47-56-52-71-00

Hammerfest Tourist Board
tel. 47-78-41-21-85

Hangen Hotel
Gamlevegen 16
N-3580 Geilo
tel. 47-32-09-06-44

Henningsvær Bryggehotel
8312 Henningsvær
tel. 47-76-07-47-50

Holmenkollen Park Hotel
Kongeveien 26
0390 Oslo
tel. 47-22-92-20-00

Hotel Ullensvang
N-5787 Lofthus
tel. 47-53-67-00-00

Norwegian Emigration Center
Strandkaien 31
N-4005 Stavanger
tel. 47-51-53-88-60
www.emigrationcenter.com

Norwegian Touring Association
tel. 47-22-82-28-22; fax 47-22-82-28-23

Rica Hotel
PO Box 463
8301 Svolvær
tel. 47-76-07-22-22

Scandinavian Tourist Board (New York)
(212) 885-9700

Sevletunet, Numedal
tel. 47-32-74-15-86

Storhaugen
tel. 47-61-21-20-69

Stryn Sommarskisenter
tel. 47-57-87-23-33

Contacts for Specialty Items

Fjord Fisheries
    137 River Road
    Cos Cob, CT 06807
    tel. 203-661-5006
    (smoked and fresh fish)

Haram-Christensen Corp.
    125 Asia Place
    Carlstadt, NJ 07072
    tel. 201-507-8544
    (Norwegian specialties like fishballs, chocolate, cheese)

Historic Edged Weaponry
    1021 Saddlebrook Drive
    Hendersonville, NC 28739
    tel. 704-692-0323
    (*lefse, surkål*, etc.)

Holbro Art Center
    7709 Fifth Avenue
    Brooklyn, NY 11209
    (Viking weapon replicas)

House of Scandinavia
    13774 South Highway 16
    Rapid City, SD 57701
    tel. 605-348-3858
    (food and supplies)

Iverson's Scandinavian Imports
    12781 Wayzata Blvd.
    Minnetonka, MN 55305
    tel. 612-545-6051
    (food items)

King's Norse Products
 3905 Dover Street
 Wheat Ridge, CO 80033
 tel. 303-422-3394
 (Norwegian delicacies, *lefse*, flatbread)

Nordic Galleri/Scandinavian Imports
 Riverfront Square
 221 W. Lincoln Ave.
 Fergus Falls, MN 56537
 (*krumkake* irons)

Nordic Ware Factory Outlet
 S.E. corner of Hwy 7 & 100
 Minneapolis, MN 55416
 tel. 800-328-4310
 (baking ware, *krumkake* irons)

Norseland Foods, Inc.
 1290 East Main Street
 Stamford, CT 06902
 tel. 203-324-5620
 (Norwegian cheeses)

Scandinavia House
 56-58 Park Avenue
 New York, NY 10016
 tel. 212-779-3587

Vanberia International Gifts
 217 W. Water Street
 PO Box 229
 Decorah, IA 52101
 tel. 800-628-5877
 (gifts and food, homemade *lefse*)

Bibliography

A History of Norway, by Karen Larsen, Princeton University Press, Princeton, New Jersey, 1950.

A History of Norwegian Literature, edited by Harald S. Naess, University of Nebraska Press, 1993.

Arctic Food, recipes by Olav Lie-Nilsen, text by Erik Jonsson Eidem, published by Eidem Forlag. Quorum Book 9.5/12 at Nikolai Olsens Trykkeri AS, Kolboth, Norway.

A Taste of Norway, produced by the Royal Ministry of Foreign Affairs in collaboration with the Royal Ministry of Agriculture.

A Time for Trolls, Fairy Tales from Norway told by Asbjørnsen and Moe. Selected and Translated with an introduction by Joan Roll-Hansen. Published by Nor-Media a.s., Oslo, 1992.

Culture Shock! A Guide to Customs and Etiquette, by Elizabeth Su-Dale, Graphic Arts Center Publishing Company, Portland, Oregon, 2000.

Guide to the History of Lofoten, Editor-in-Chief Gro Rode, published with the Lofoten Public Museums, Lofoten Regional Council, 1996.

Jakt I Norge, Direktoratet for naturforvaltning, Adresseavisen Offset AS.

Milestones of Norwegian Literature, by Tørbjørn Støverud, Johan Grundt Tanum Forlag, Oslo, 1967.

News of Norway, Feb. 2000, March 2000, Issued by the Royal Norwegian Embassy, Washington, D.C.

Norway, by Barbara Øvstedal, B. T. Batsford Ltd, London, 1973.

Norway Information Bulletins, produced by the Ministry of Foreign Affairs by Nytt fra Norge: "A Taste of Norway"; "Norse Mythology" by Tor Åge Bringsværd, October 1994; "Norwegian Food" by Brita Drangsholt Jaksjø, September 1994; "The 17th of May" by Knut Mykland, March 1996; "Christmas in Norway," by Vera Henriksen, March 1996; "The Stave Churches of Norway" by Håkon Christie, March 1996.

Norway's Delight, by Elise Sverdrup, published by Johan Grundt Tanum Forlag, Oslo, 1957.

Norway: The Rough Guide, by Phil Lee, The Rough Guides, 2000.

Norway Times, Dec. 14, 1995, Dec. 12, 1996 (No. 46), March 8, 2000 (No. 10), May 11, 2000 (No. 19), Sept. 21 2000 (No. 34).

Norwegian Literature 1993, The Norseman, vol. 33, No. 4/5, Editor Johan Fr. Heyerdahl.

Open City, "We are flames which pour out of the earth: Introduction to the Journals of Edvard Munch" by Gill Holland, Number Nine, New York, Fall 1999, p. 243.

The Norseman, "Pride in the Norwegian Kitchen" translated by Ann Clay Zwick, Nordmanns-Forbunnet, No. 2 March 1996, pp. 41–44.

The Romantic 90s, by Richard Le Gallienne, Garden City, New York. Doubleday, Page & Company 1926; pp 68–79.

This Is Norway, "A Thousand Years of Norwegian Food" by Henry Notaker, Edited by Arne Bonde, J.M. Stenersens Forlag AS, Oslo, 1992.

Viking, October 2000 (Vol. 97, No. 9), December 2000 (Vol. 97, No. 11), published by Sons of Norway, Minneapolis, Minnesota.

Viking Cookbook, Egmont Boker Fredhoi AS-SPG, Oslo.

Visitor's Guide Norway, World Traveller Series, by Don Philpott, MPC Hunter Publishing,1991.

Index

Norwegian-interest titles from Hippocrene...

Norse Stories

Retold by Hamilton Wright Mabie
Illustrated by George Wright

"These ancient books, which a brave and noble race carried in its heart through all its wide wanderings and conquests, take one back to the beginning of the worlds and the coming of the gods to rule over them ..."

Thus begins the first story, "The Making of the World," in this unique illustrated collection of Norse myths and stories. Originally published in 1901, this rare volume of 17 stories has been brought back into print by Hippocrene Books one hundred years later. Stories of brave warriors, fierce gods, and exciting adventures included in such tales as "Odin's Search for Wisdom," "Thor Goes a Fishing," "How Thor Fought the Giant Hrungner" and "The Twilight of the Gods" will enchant children and adults alike.

250 pages • 5½ x 8¼ • illustrations • ISBN 0-7818-0770-0 • $14.95hc • (357)

Hippocrene Children's Illustrated Norwegian Dictionary
English-Norwegian/Norwegian-English

- for ages 5 and up
- 500 entries with color pictures
- commonsense pronunciation for each Norwegian word
- Norwegian-English index

94 pages • 8 x 11½ • ISBN 0-7818-0887-1 • $11.95pb • (165)

Norwegian-English/English-Norwegian
Concise Dictionary

10,000 entries • 599 pages • 4 x 6 • ISBN 0-7818-0199-0 • $14.95pb • (202)

Mastering Norwegian
Erik Friis

183 pages • 5½ x 8½ • ISBN 0-7818-0320-9 • $14.95pb • (472)

Scandinavian-interest titles from Hippocrene . . .

COOKBOOKS

The Best of Scandinavian Cooking: Danish, Norwegian and Swedish
Shirley Sarvis & Barbara Scott O'Neil

This exciting collection of 100 recipes, each dish the favorite of a Scandinavian cook, spans the range of home cooking—appetizers, soups, omelets, pancakes, meats and pastries. Included are directions for making such tempting dishes as Norwegian Blueberry Omelet, Danish Butter Cake, Swedish Pancakes with Ligonberries—and a section entitled "A Smørrebrød Sampling," devoted to those open-faced Danish sandwiches. Each recipe has been carefully tested with North American ingredients and measures.

142 pages • 5½ x 8¼ • ISBN 0-7818-0547-3 • $9.95pb • (643)

Icelandic Food & Cookery
Nanna Rögnvaldardóttir

More than just 165 recipes for classic Icelandic dishes, this cookbook explores the evolution of Icelandic cuisine over the last two centuries. From the late 19th century until the 1970s, thick meat stews, roasts, porridges, milk and fruit soups, and various cakes and pastries were popular. More modern trends include making use of the wonderful fresh fish and shellfish in Icelandic waters, sweet-tasting Icelandic lamb, game birds, and local wild herbs. The author includes favorites that have endured through the years and the best of recent dishes that still reflect Icelandic ingredients and cooking methods. Sample such delicacies as "Iceland Moss Soup," "Grilled Rosemary-Flavored Char," "Braised Wild Goose with Fruit Stuffing," and "Bilberry Ice Cream." Home chefs will welcome the helpful chapters on Festive Food Traditions and Icelandic Ingredients.

158 pages • 5½ x 8½ • ISBN 0-7818-0878-2 • $24.95hc • (12)

Good Food from Sweden
Inga Norberg

This classic of Swedish cookery includes recipes for fish and meat dishes, vegetables, breads and sweets, including cookies, cakes candies and syrups. A large section is dedicated to the savory tidbits included in the traditional Swedish smorgasbord.

192 pages • 5½ x 8¼ • ISBN 0-7818-0486-8 • $10.95pb • (544)

The Best of Smorgasbord Cooking
Gerda Simonson

Recipes for the traditional Swedish smorgasbord, including meat and game dishes, aspics and salads, fish, pastas and vegetables.

158 pages • 5½ x 8¼ • ISBN 0-7818-0407-8 • $14.95pb • (207)

The Best of Finnish Cooking
Taimi Previdi

"Over 200 recipes are relatively easy to follow . . . from meat pies and beef stews to puddings and casseroles."
—*The Midwest Book Review*

"The book is divided clearly into sections of different menu items and the directions are detailed . . . *The Best of Finnish Cooking* is a good and practical cookbook. It makes a wonderful Christmas gift for people interested in cooking or things Finnish."
—*Amerikan Uutiset*

The Finnish-born author has compiled a delicious array of recipes for every occasion:

- Authentic Finnish recipes, adapted for the American kitchen.
- Traditional recipes for main courses, soups, salads, appetizers, sandwiches and desserts.
- Delicious baking recipes for breads (both sweet and savory), cakes and cookies.
- Menus for special holidays, such as Easter, Midsummer and Christmas.
- Finnish names for recipes and an index in Finnish and English.

242 pages • 5½ x 8½ • ISBN 0-7818-0493-0 • $12.95pb • (601)

POETRY AND FOLKLORE

Treasury of Finnish Love Poems, Quotations & Proverbs In Finnish and English
Börje Vähämäki, *editor and translator*

128 pages • 5 x 7 • ISBN 0-7818-0397-7 • $11.95hc • (118)

Swedish Fairy Tales
Translated by H. L. Braekstad

A unique blend of enchantment, adventure, comedy, and romance make this collection of Swedish fairy tales a must-have for any library. With 18 different, classic Swedish fairy tales and 21 beautiful black-and-white illustrations, this is an ideal gift for children and adults alike.

190 pages • 5½ x 8½ • 21 b/w illustrations • ISBN 0-7818-0717-4 • $12.50hc • (787)

The Little Mermaid and Other Tales
Hans Christian Andersen

This beautiful collection of 27 stories from the Danish master of fairy tales, Hans Christian Andersen, whisks the reader to magical lands, fantastic voyages, romantic encounters and adventures. Children and adults alike will enjoy timeless favorites including "The Little Mermaid," "The Emperor's New Clothes," "The Little Match-girl," and "The Ugly Duckling." Stunningly illustrated throughout, this is a near replica of the first American edition of the collection.

508 pages • 6⅛ x 9¼ • illustrations throughout • ISBN 0-7818-0720-4 • $19.95hc • (791)

SCANDINAVIAN LANGUAGES

Hippocrene Children's Illustrated Swedish Dictionary
English-Swedish/Swedish-English
  • for ages 5 and up
  • 500 entries with color pictures
  • commonsense pronunciation for each Swedish word
  • Swedish-English index

Hardcover: 94 pages • 8½ x 11 • ISBN 0-7818-0822-7 • $14.95hc • (57)
Paperback: 94 pages • 8½ x 11 • ISBN 0-7818-0850-2 • $11.95pb • (665)

Swedish-English/English-Swedish
Dictionary and Phrasebook
Julie Hansen and Dick Nilsson

This dictionary and phrasebook is an essential resource for visitors to the land of Ingmar Bergman, Ikea, ABBA, the Nobel Prizes, Absolut Vodka, and Pippi Longstocking. A pronunciation guide and a grammar section ensure that users understand the structure of Swedish, while important contextual information will help travelers avoid embarrassing moments! The two-way dictionary totals 3,000 entries, and the phrasebook contains more than 20 sections ranging from introductions to shopping to weights & measures (with conversion chart).

3,000 entries • 152 pages • 3¾ x 7½ • ISBN 0-7818-0903-7 • $11.95pb • (228)

Swedish-English/English-Swedish Standard Dictionary

70,000 entries • 804 pages • 5½ x 8½ • ISBN 0-7818-0379-9 • $19.95pb • (242)

Finnish-English/English-Finnish Concise Dictionary

12,000 entries • 411 pages • 3½ x 4¾ • ISBN 0-87052-813-0 • $11.95pb • (142)

Danish-English/English-Danish Practical Dictionary

32,000 entries • 601 pages • 4⅜ x 7 • ISBN 0-87052-823-8 • $16.95pb • (198)

Icelandic-English/English-Icelandic Concise Dictionary

10,000 entries • 177 pages • 4 x 6 • ISBN 0-87052-801-7 • $9.95pb • (147)

All prices subject to change without prior notice. **To purchase Hippocrene Books** contact your local bookstore, call (718) 454-2366, or write to: HIPPOCRENE BOOKS, 171 Madison Avenue, New York, NY 10016. Please enclose check or money order, adding $5.00 shipping (UPS) for the first book and $.50 for each additional book.